KT-210-390

25 WALKS

HEART
OF
SCOTLAND

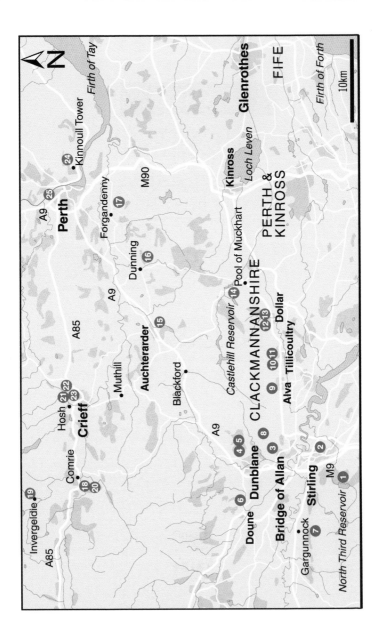

25 WALKS

HEART OF SCOTLAND

ROGER SMITH

SERIES EDITOR: ROGER SMITH

MERCAT

First published in 2008 by Mercat Press, an imprint of Birlinn Ltd,
West Newington House, 10 Newington Road
Edinburgh EH9 1QS
www.birlinn.co.uk

© Roger Smith, 2008

All photographs © Roger Smith
Cartography by Allyson Hasson

ISBN 13: 978-1-84183-115-2

Maps reproduced by permission of Ordnance Survey
© Crown Copyright 2007
Ordnance Survey Licence number 100031557

Printed and bound in Britain by Bell & Bain Ltd, Glasgow

CONTENTS

PRACTICAL INFORMATION

The length of each walk is given in kilometres and miles, but within the text, measurements are metric for simplicity. The walks are described in detail and are supported by specially prepared maps with the route marked out, which you should study before you start the walk. There should be little chance of going astray, but if you want a back-up, take an Ordnance Survey 1:50000 Landranger or 1:25000 Explorer map with you. The maps are at various scales, but in every case the scale is marked on the individual map.

Every care has been taken to make the walk descriptions and maps as accurate as possible, but the author and publishers can accept no responsibility for errors, however caused. The countryside is always changing and there will inevitably be alterations to some aspects of these walks as time passes. The publishers and author would be happy to receive comments and suggested alterations for future editions of the book (see below).

Access in Scotland

The Land Reform Act came into full effect in Scotland in February 2005. The Act gives the public a general right of access to all open countryside in Scotland, with the proviso that this access must be exercised responsibly. There are exceptions to the general right such as in the vicinity of houses or other buildings, on industrial sites, airports and railway lines, and military areas. Access rights can be temporarily suspended for activities such as shooting or timber felling.

The rights and responsibilities of the public and of land managers are explained in the Scottish Outdoor Access Code which can be found at: www.outdooraccess-scotland.com. Simplified versions of the Code are available in leaflet form (Know the Code Before You Go) at Tourist Information Centres or from Scottish Natural Heritage (www.snh.gov.uk). The principal points emphasised in the Code are as follows:

- Take personal responsibility for your own actions, and act safely
- Respect people's privacy and peace of mind
- Help land managers and others to work safely and effectively
- Care for your environment and take your litter home
- Keep your dog under proper control
- Take extra care if you are organising an event or running a business.

Most of the walks in this book are along well-established routes and there should be no difficulties encountered. All routes have been agreed with landowners or land managers where this was thought necessary, and we are grateful for their co-operation and their interest in the book.

Dogs and Livestock

Dogs must always be kept under close control in the countryside, and we recommend that dogs are not taken on walks in livestock areas, and particularly not during lambing and calving times (notably in the spring between March and May).

A number of the walks in this book pass through livestock areas where sheep or cattle may be encountered. This should not cause any particular problem, but again, please go quietly in these areas and take every care not to disturb livestock, on which the farmer's livelihood depends.

Gates

The general advice with farm gates is to leave them as you find them. If a gate is closed, shut it carefully and securely behind you. Please be scrupulous about this: carelessly leaving a gate open may lead to stock getting into the wrong field and cause the farmer a great deal of difficulty. It also gives walkers a bad name. If a gate is open, this is for a reason, and it should be left open.

Litter

We do ask walkers to be absolutely scrupulous about not leaving litter, and indeed to help reduce this pernicious problem by picking up litter that others have left. Your help in this is much appreciated.

General Information

Information on the area covered in this book can be obtained via the websites at www.visitscottishheartlands.com and www.perthshire. co.uk where you will find clear links to the area, these in turn leading to more detailed information. You can also try the VisitScotland information line on 0845 22 55 121.

The main tourist information centres for the area are as shown below. These TICs are open all year.

- Lower City Mills, West Mill Street, Perth PH1 5QP
  perthtic@perthshire.co.uk
- 41 Dumbarton Road, Stirling FK8 2QQ
  info@visitscotland.com

There is also a seasonal TIC at Stirling Road, Dunblane FK15 9EP (May-Sept), email: info@dunblane.visitscotland.com and there are TICs at the Mill Trail Visitor Centre in Alva and at the Pirnhall Services on the M9/M80 near Stirling

Countryside and access information is also available through the websites of Stirling Council at www.stirling.gov.uk, Perth & Kinross Council at www.perthandkinross.gov.uk and Clackmannanshire Council at www.clackmannan.gov.uk.

There are forest walks in the area and details can be obtained from the Forestry Commission, Perth & Argyll Conservancy, Algo Business Centre, Glenearn Road, Perth PH2 0NJ, phone 01738 442830, email panda.cons@forestry.gsi.gov.uk.

Information and contact details specific to particular walks are given in the information panel for that walk, as are details for any relevant community or local websites.

Public transport

We wish to encourage walkers to use buses and trains whenever possible, and most of the walks in this book are easily accessible by public transport. The networks are indeed excellent in this area. Details of bus services can be obtained through tourist information centres, from the bus stations in Stirling and Perth, or via the national Traveline on 0870 608 2 608 or www.travelinescotland.com, which contains full timetable information. Some bus services do not run or may have reduced frequency on Sundays: check your information before setting out.

There are rail stations at Stirling, Bridge of Allan, Dunblane, Gleneagles and Perth, with frequent services from Edinburgh and Glasgow. For details of services contact the national rail enquiry line on 08457 48 49 50, go to www.firstgroup.com/scotrail or enquire at stations.

Information updates

All information provided in this book is believed to be accurate at the time of going to print. However, things inevitably change and we would be grateful for any advice as to alterations or amendments for future editions. Please write to Mercat Press, Birlinn Ltd, West Newington House, 10 Newington Road, Edinburgh EH9 1QS, or email us via www.birlinn.co.uk.

A shaded path in Hermitage Wood, Bridge of Allan (Walk 3)

INTRODUCTION

The gestation for this book came when (in my role as Series Editor) I was looking at a map of Scotland and assessing our coverage. There appeared to be an intriguing-looking gap between the Central Belt, Fife and Highland Perthshire. As soon as I started doing a little research, I realised that this gap was full of good walks and could provide the opportunity for a very interesting book.

The book covers a broad area of countryside either side of the A9 road, roughly between Stirling and Perth. 'Heart of Scotland' seemed a very appropriate title, and indeed the phrase has been used as a slogan by the former Perthshire Tourist Board. The area has a fine city at each end and is characterised by attractive countryside with rolling hills, beautiful rivers and a wealth of history. It has been strategically significant throughout the whole of Scotland's history, going back over two thousand years to the time when the extraordinary hill forts were constructed.

There are a number of very pleasant towns and villages which are used as bases for many of the walks. These places, such as Dunblane, Kippen, Tillicoultry, Comrie and Crieff, are all enjoyable to visit and offer good facilities for pre- or post-walk refreshments.

In addition, the three local authorities covering the book's scope (Clackmannanshire, Stirling, and Perth & Kinross Councils) have all been proactive in creating path networks, and this process will continue and expand as the new access legislation in Scotland comes into full effect over the next 5-10 years.

Many of the walks in the book are thus well known. However, I was not content simply to borrow walks that others had created. There are a number of less well-known walks included, such as Craig Rossie and Pitcairns Den, and I have also combined the best bits of existing walks to make them (in my view, anyway!) even better, as in the two circuits of Crieff and the lovely walk along the Hillfoots towns and villages.

I was not far into the book before two distinct themes began to emerge. The first of these is strongholds. This is not surprising, given the importance of the area's through routes linking Lowlands and Highlands. However, I was able to include not only the big 'showpiece'

Triple-armed signpost on the Darn Road near Dunblane (Walk 4)

castles such as Stirling, Doune and Castle Campbell, but also some lesser-known examples and also several ancient hillforts. In terms of the labour that went into their construction, given their antiquity, I find these places simply magical. Castle Law is a superb example, if it does take a little imagination to see all of its complexities.

The second major theme was water. The area is not noted for its lochs, and the best of these, Airthrey on the Stirling University campus, is manmade, but the rivers are just glorious. You have the opportunity to walk beside the Earn, the Almond, the Allan Water and others, and of course the mighty Tay and Forth, two of Scotland's longest and finest.

As well as this, the book includes the intricate Town Lade in Perth and a number of lovely smaller streams.

The book includes a number of very attractive hills of modest height. Dumyat, at the western end of the Ochils, is rightly popular, but Craig Rossie, Seamab and Lewis Hill are less well-known. They all fully merit inclusion. All give great views (on a clear day, of course!) for relatively little effort in reaching their summits.

The two higher hills in the book are Ben Cleuch and Ben Chonzie. Ben Cleuch is the highest point of the Ochils, at 721m, but the circuit described here also takes in the Law above Tillicoultry and includes fine woodland. Ben Chonzie is included to give readers the chance to bag a relatively straightforward Munro (the generic name for Scotland's 3000-foot hills). I climbed it most recently on the exact 150th anniversary of Sir Hugh Munro's birth in October 1856, which seemed fitting.

Most of the walks in the book are circular. Five are linear, but in each case there is a good public transport link back to the start. The longest of the linear walks, the old right of way across the Ochils from Tillicoultry to Blackford, provides an interesting, but not difficult, exercise in logistics. It can easily be done from Stirling using buses, and I would encourage readers to try this method. Public transport information is provided for each walk. Nearly all of them are readily accessible by bus, and quite a few have rail links too. If, like me, you have passed 60 and live in Scotland, you have the gift of free bus travel, a privilege I fully exploited while research, and walking the routes in the book.

The walks in this book provide tremendous variety and pass through some of Scotland's most beautiful countryside. Hills, rivers, woods, villages and much more are here for you to savour. Putting the book together was hugely enjoyable and satisfying, and my hope is that you, the reader, will get as much pleasure from these walks as I have.

Roger Smith, February 2008

Acknowledgements

Many people helped in the preparation of this book, and this help is gratefully acknowledged. They include the University of Stirling (Bridge of Allan walk); Mr and Mrs Mitchell, Pairney Farm (Craig Rossie); Lord Rollo (Pitcairns Den); Mr Hans-Jurgen Queisser, Glenearn (Castle Law); the Woodland Trust, Auchterarder (Seamab Hill); Richard Barron, Access Officer, Stirling Council; Dave Stubbs, Access Officer, Perth & Kinross Council; and Perth & Kinross Council Library Service Archives Department. I would also like to thank my wife Patricia and daughter Becky, who accompanied me on a number of the walks and provided extremely valuable advice as independent walks assessors. If they thought the walk was good, it went in!

My apologies to anyone I may have inadvertently omitted from this list, and also for any errors or omissions in the text. I am always pleased to hear from readers with constructive comments or criticism.

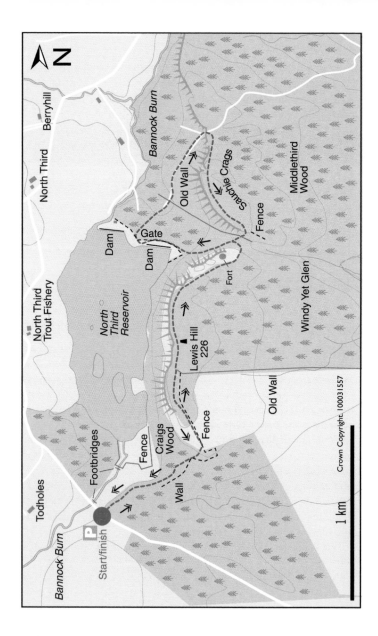

LEWIS HILL AND NORTH THIRD

Distance	6km (4 miles) circular.
Ascent	300 metres approx.
Start and finish	Small layby on minor road near North Third Reservoir (GR 758880), just south of the bridge over the Bannock Burn. To get there, turn off the A872 at the Bannockburn Heritage Centre and take the first left, signed for North Third. Follow this road for about 5km, then turn right for North Third. In 1.5km, the road descends steeply. The layby is at the edge of the wood.
Terrain	Hill paths. Boots recommended.
Map	Free North Third footpaths map available locally.
Public transport	None to the start.
Refreshments	None on route. Nearest in Stirling.
Toilets	None on route.
Opening hours	**Bannockburn Heritage Centre**: Apr-Oct, daily 10.30-17.30. Feb-Mar, Nov-Dec, daily 10.30-16.00. Closed Jan. *Note:* **The path is close to the edge of the crags at several points. Please take extra care, especially with children or dogs.**

This is a spectacular little walk. Don't be fooled by the short distance. There are several stiff ascents and it makes a good outing. While the paths are in reasonable condition, after rain some of the descents can be slippery and need a little care.

Your first challenge is finding the start, but assuming you have done so, follow the waymark arrow into the woods, immediately climbing quite steeply. This is Craigs Wood and has a real mixture of trees, including some venerable oaks and beeches. At the top of the first bank, keep left with dark conifers to the right. Follow the path across a gully, then climb again, keeping an eye out for the markers. You soon get your first view of the reservoir to the left.

At a path junction, turn left along the edge of the wood, passing some superb old trees. Continue climbing steadily, then more gently, with a fence on the right. Reach the edge of the crags and follow the path up to Lewis Hill. Just before the final short climb there is a great

North Third Reservoir dam

view ahead past the crags to the reservoir dam and beyond to the rank of hills including Ben Ledi. The Braes of Doune wind farm also stands out.

The trig pillar on Lewis Hill, though only at 266m, commands a superb panorama. The reservoir, usually busy with fishermen, is directly below, and the skyline takes in a wide range of hills. Looking back you can see Loch Coulter, another reservoir. It is definitely a place to linger on a fine day. The crags drop very steeply away from the edge so do take care as you continue along the path. Another lovely view opens up, this time including the Wallace Monument below Dumyat.

The path starts to descend, gently at first then more steeply round a series of zigzags to the pass below, which has the evocative name of Windy Yett ('yett' means a gate, but is often applied to a pass in the hills). Take care going down the zigzags as the path is rough and steep here.

At the foot of the zig-zags, turn left with the arrow, along the edge of the wood. Sheer crags rear up impressively to the right. The path drops to run below the dam, then swings right to a metal gate. Turn right here on a path which leads to a forest road. (If you go through the gate you can walk over to the dam for a fine view of the reservoir. North Third was built in 1931 as part of the public water supply system.)

Follow the forest road gently uphill, then (past a turnoff) more steeply. Watch for a marker on the right and take the path here to start climbing back above Sauchie Craigs. In about 100m, turn right as signed. The path descends briefly before climbing again, very steeply, on a rough section which can be slippery if wet. Please take extra care here.

Cross a gully and continue along the crags, with the path very near to the edge. Birdlife in this area includes ravens, kestrels and buzzards, and if you are lucky you might spot a flash of white rump as a roe deer bounds away through the woods.

You are now almost level with Lewis Hill, but have to drop and reascend quite a way, unfortunately! The path makes a steady descent around several bends to reach the foot of the zig-zags. From here you retrace your outward route, back over Lewis Hill and down through Craigs Wood to the start.

Take your time and savour the views. There are some fine old birches beside the path on the way up the hill and you can enjoy looking down at the anglers far below you. On the 'nose' of the hill to the right of the zig-zags as you climb was an Iron Age fort, in a wonderful defensive setting. At that time, of course, there was no reservoir, just the Bannock Burn meandering quietly through the marshes. The burn, which was to play such a significant part in Scottish history with the battle of 1314, is still there, and a visit to the Bannockburn Heritage Centre, which tells the story of Robert the Bruce and the battle, would round off your day nicely.

The summit of Lewis Hill

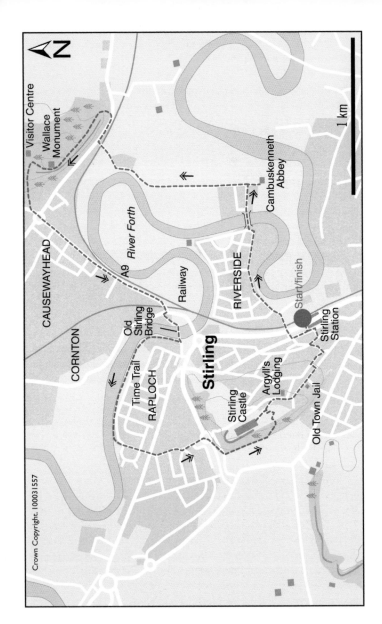

HISTORIC STIRLING

Distance	10km (6 miles) circular.
Start and finish	Stirling Railway Station (ample parking nearby).
Terrain	Road, tracks and good paths. Boots only needed in wet conditions.
Map	Stirling Walks leaflet available locally.
Public transport	Regular trains and buses to Stirling from Glasgow, Edinburgh, Perth and other main centres.
Refreshments	Wide choice in Stirling. Inn in Cambuskenneth. Café at the Wallace Monument.
Toilets	At the start and at the Wallace Monument.
Opening hours	**Cambuskenneth Abbey** (Historic Scotland): Apr-Sep Mon-Sat 9.30am-6pm; Sun 2pm-6pm. **National Wallace Monument:** Open all year daily. Times vary. **Stirling Castle** (HS): Apr-Oct, daily 9.30am-6pm; Nov-Mar daily 9.30am-5pm. **Argyll's Lodging** (HS): as the Castle. **Old Town Jail:** Apr-Sep 9.30am-6pm; Oct-Mar 9.30am-5pm.

This walk takes you to a number of wonderful sites and monuments. It also provides surprisingly quiet riverside and woodland walking at times. There is so much to see that you could easily spend a whole day on the walk. The route includes an intriguing 'timeline' path, but in fact the whole walk can be seen as a timeline which helps to tell the story of Stirling's (and Scotland's) past. Stirling has been called 'the clasp at Scotland's waist', and its strategic position means that it has been at the heart of matters both spiritual and secular for nearly a thousand years.

Turn right out of the station and right again to cross the road and railway. There is already a good view of Dumyat and the Ochils. Keep left at the roundabout and follow the path to cross a grassy area by the River Forth. This was the site of the old Stirling Harbour in the 17th century.

Rejoin the pavement (NCR76 sign) into Abbey Road. Follow the road round to the left and cross the river by the footbridge into the attractive village of Cambuskenneth. 'Cambus' means a bend in a river. At the junction, turn right to Cambuskenneth Abbey. It was started in 1140 by King David I, at the time the first fortifications up at

Cambuskenneth Abbey

the castle were being developed, and was an Augustinian foundation. It was largely dismantled after the Reformation in 1560. The impressive tower was restored in the 1860s. It is a beautiful and peaceful place.

Return along the road with the Castle visible up to the left, and once you leave the houses behind, a very impressive view of the Wallace Monument on Abbey Craig ahead, with Dumyat to its right. The 'crag and tail' volcanic formation is clear. The river joins at the left. At the 30mph sign, turn right on a path (an old road). Continue across the railway. This is the line from Stirling to Alloa, and at the time of publication, was being restored for passenger traffic.

Turn right on the road and once past the buildings, take the path on the left (at a stone step) and start climbing. Turn left on another path and continue to climb through mature woodland including oaks, sycamores and pines. You will almost certainly see squirrels. Keep on the main path, up steps and continue climbing to reach a viewpoint looking across the remarkable convolutions of the Forth to Stirling and beyond. Abbey Craig, like the Castle Rock, is a volcanic plug made of harder rock than the surrounding area.

Continue with the path to the National Wallace Monument. The 75m tower was built in 1869 and at the time was highly controversial. It has long since been accepted as part of the landscape. It houses exhibitions on the life of William Wallace, and the view from the top is breathtaking.

Take the path beyond the monument, down rough steps which need a little care, to the access road. Turn left and walk down to the visitor centre with its striking statue of Wallace by Tom Church. To continue the walk, go back up the road a short way and take the path running down by the wall on the right. Continue parallel to the wall to reach a long flight of steep steps. Take care down these steps, and use the handrail.

Cross the open area past play equipment and turn right on the road. Turn left at the roundabout (Causewayhead Road). This is a slightly tedious link section, but is needed to get us back towards Stirling. Cross the road halfway along to stay on the pavement, pass Bridgehaugh, the home of Stirling County RFC, and go under the railway. Cross the road at the lights and continue to Old Stirling Brig.

Old Stirling Brig

WALK 2

7

This lovely old 15th-century bridge is now only used by pedestrians and cyclists, but at one time was a vital crossing point, the last on the Forth, with none further downriver. Its wooden predecessor was the key to the Battle of Stirling Brig in 1297, possibly Wallace's finest victory, and one which paved the way for Bruce's triumph at Bannockburn in 1314.

At the far side of the bridge, turn right down to the riverside path and turn left. Follow the path along, with the river on your right. The path features a 'timeline' with a series of inscriptions taking us from the Battle of Bannockburn through the formation of the village of Raploch, on to the Jacobite Rebellions, and right up to 2006 when the timeline was opened. It adds considerable interest to the walk as you follow the path round with the houses of modern Raploch ('place of archers') to the left.

When the road bends left, fork left past a play area and join Woodside Road. Cross into Glendevon Drive, where a large housing development is under way. The castle looms imposingly ahead. Pass Raploch Community Centre and go up to Back o' Hill Road. Cross right of the roundabout and take the signposted path to start climbing through the trees.

At a road, cross and take the path signposted for Royal Gardens. Follow this path along, with the formal landscaping known as the King's Knot ahead. Fork left, up through a gap in the wall, and then take the steep path going up left by zig-zags and old steps. This path leads to a junction. Turn right and at the cemetery turn left. Cross another path and go up steps to the Castle Esplanade.

Stirling Castle is in fact a substantial complex of buildings, including the castle fortifications, the Great Hall (the largest in Scotland), the Chapel Royal where Mary, Queen of Scots was crowned in 1543, and the Renaissance Royal Palace built for King James V in 1538. Tours, displays and exhibitions tell a fuller story.

Follow the cobbled access road down, passing Argyll's Lodging, one of the finest 17th-century town houses in Scotland. Pass the Church of the Holy Rude, where James VI was crowned in 1567, and keep right to the Old Town Jail, which offers a fascinating 'living history' experience presented by actors, showing how hard life was for Victorian criminals. Pass the 1740 Erskine Church and go left and right into Baker Street. Go left on Friars Street with its intriguing variety of shops. There is much more to see in Stirling than can be described here.

Turn right on Murray Place and then left, back to the station.

BRIDGE OF ALLAN

Distance	7km (4.5 miles) circular.
Start and finish	Fountain Road car park, Bridge of Allan (the walk could also be started from Bridge of Allan Station).
Terrain	Road, tracks and generally good paths. Boots recommended.
Map	Free Bridge of Allan path leaflet available locally.
Public transport	Frequent trains to Bridge of Allan from Glasgow and Edinburgh. Frequent buses from Stirling.
Refreshments	Reasonable choice in Bridge of Allan.
Toilets	Henderson Street.

This walk includes some fine mature woodland and part of the attractive campus of Stirling University.

From the car park, turn left up to Henderson Street, cross and turn left. The Royal Hotel has plaques noting some of its distinguished visitors, including Charles Dickens and Robert Louis Stevenson. Pass the Provost's Lamp. At one time all provosts of the town were given a lamp like this outside their houses during their term of office.

Turn right on to Well Road, noting the striking mural on the wall of the toilets. Created by Isobel Hamilton in 2002, it depicts local scenes and people associated with the town. Curve right, still on Well Road, and climb steadily. Turn left on Sunnylaw Road. At its end, cross and go up steps on to the Coppermine Path in Mine Wood. Copper was indeed mined here, though only on a small scale, until about 1810.

This lovely path climbs steadily through fine mature woodland, traversing a long flight of steps then passing along a shelf on the hillside. Past a seat keep left, still uphill, with more steps. It's a fair climb so take your time. The surroundings are very attractive and there are plenty of woodland birds.

Continue climbing with the path to reach a minor road at a signpost. Turn right on the road (you can walk just inside the wood for the first bit). Pass Drumbrae Farm and Riding Centre, with Dumyat peeping its head over the buildings to the left. There is a terrific view across the University campus to the Wallace Monument straight ahead, and

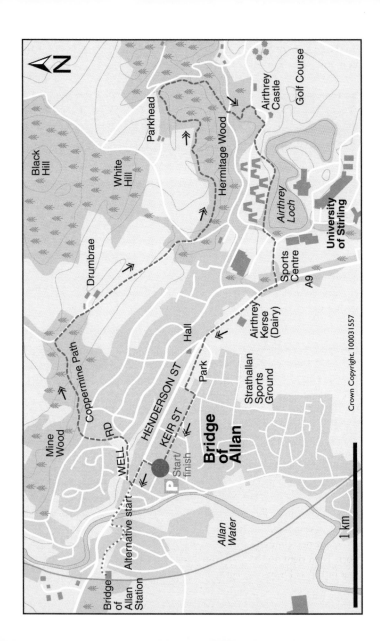

Crown Copyright. 100031557

on the far right of the skyline, in clear conditions, you can pick out Ben Lomond.

Continue down the road into woodland. Just after a road joins from the left, go up steps through the wall on the left into Hermitage Wood. Take the path ahead of you, climbing gently through mature trees. This excellent path keeps high through the wood, at one point dropping a little to cross a rather boggy area before climbing again, close to a fence and wall with Parkhead Farm to the left.

Swing left at the wall corner, then right, gently downhill. Near here is the Hermitage, after which the wood is named. It's an old ruined stone structure, rather overgrown. See if you can find it.

At the junction go left on the broad path then go sharp right with the Logie Kirk Road on your left. Keep on this path, which goes steadily downhill. Join a fence past a covered reservoir then swing right with the path to reach a junction with a track (called Back o' Dykes) at a triple signpost.

Cross the track and in 50 metres go right, down to a road. This path is part of the Joyce Dunn Walk, named for the founder and former chair of the Airthrey Gardens Group. Turn left along the road, and at the junction go right, past Airthrey Castle and into the main part of the university campus. It is very attractively landscaped with plenty of open space. The estate was laid out by Thomas White for the Haldane family in the late 18th century, and the castle was designed by Robert Adam. The University took it over in the 1960s and it opened to students in 1967.

Keep right, following the path by the road, and then take the first path on the left, leading down to Airthrey Loch. Turn right on the lochside path and follow it again, passing the bridge which leads over to the MacRobert Arts Centre. You are now on a broad surfaced path. There is usually a good variety of waterfowl on the loch, which at one time was used for curling. Many of the trees and shrubs have been planted by the Airthrey Gardens Group. In spring there are lovely displays of daffodils.

Turn left when you meet a road. There is a great view looking down the loch to Airthrey Castle and the Wallace Monument. Turn right on the path beside the main driveway and walk out to the A9. Cross the road with care and turn right.

Airthrey Loch

Pass Airthrey Kerse Dairy, cross Keir Street and take the path through the park. There are lovely trees here including cherry and maple. Across the road is the Museum Hall, a listed building whose future has been the subject of a long debate. The Beatles played here at a very early stage of their career — and were apparently booed off.

To return to the car park, go left on Graham Street and right on Keir Street. If you are going back to the station, simply continue along Henderson Street, named for the Victorian landowner who greatly encouraged the development of the town. At one time Bridge of Allan had pretensions to be a spa, and the old Pump Room can still be seen in Chalton Road.

WALK 3

THE DARN ROAD

Distance	10.5km (6.5 miles) circular.
Start and finish	Dunblane Station (the walk could also be started from any of the car parks in the town).
Terrain	Road, tracks and generally good paths. Boots recommended.
Map	Free Dunblane path leaflet available locally.
Public transport	Frequent trains to Dunblane from Glasgow, Edinburgh and Perth.
Refreshments	Good choice in Dunblane and Bridge of Allan.
Toilets	Near the start and close to the cathedral.
Further information	If you visit *www.dunblaneweb.co.uk* you can find out much more about the town and the area. You can also pick up an excellent Historic Town Trail leaflet locally. There is a seasonal Tourist Information Centre (open April-October) near the station.

This figure-of-eight walk links Dunblane with Bridge of Allan through a historic route and includes superb woodland and fine open countryside.

From the station, walk down Stirling Road past the TIC and cross the Allan Water. This is the Nether Port, and there has been a bridge here for over 500 years. Pass the Stirling Arms Hotel (1770) and turn right. Cross the road at the top, and just to the left you will see the start of the path, with an old signpost.

This is the Darn Road, an ancient right of way between Dunblane and Bridge of Allan. The path initially follows the edge of Dunblane Golf Course. The Keir Estate woods to the right contain many fine old trees including pines and beeches.

Before long the path enters woodland at a massive old oak tree. There are also tall, graceful birches. Cross more open ground, walking between a fence and a wall with overhanging trees. Some of the oldest larches in Scotland are in this area. The larch was introduced to Scotland in 1738 from Austria, and has flourished here ever since.

The path, now quite stony, runs gently downhill. Re-enter the woods, the path becoming broader and smoother under heavy tree cover. There are more lovely old trees in this area.

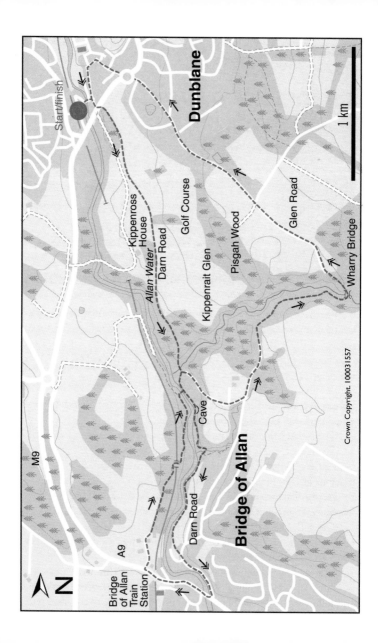

The Darn Road near Dunblane

Reach the strong footbridge over the Wharry Burn at a triple-armed signpost, and continue ahead following the signs for Bridge of Allan. In about 150 metres you reach a bridge over the Allan Water. Don't cross it – this is the return route – but continue with the Darn Road path beside the rushing water.

Before long you reach Robert Louis Stevenson's 'cave' (more of a rocky recess) which the author said 'has been part of me these past 12 years or so'. It is said he drew inspiration for Ben Gunn's Cave in *Treasure Island* while sitting here.

The path cuts back to the left to cross Cock's Burn in a beautiful miniature gorge, rich with ferns. A short climb restores the path to its previous level, well above the river. The first houses on the outskirts of Bridge of Allan are seen, and the path runs beside fields where inquisitive horses may come looking for food. It is better not to indulge them.

The path becomes surfaced and reaches a road. Turn right, downhill, and at the main road turn right (or left if you want to get refreshments). Cross the Allan Water, noting on the left a house with a redundant waterwheel. There were once several mills in this area.

Just past Lecropt Nursery, turn right (footpath sign to Dunblane) and follow the road up, then take the path at the side of the last house

WALK 4

15

(Milseybank). The path leads gently uphill through more beautiful woodland where you may see rabbits, squirrels or perhaps a roe deer, or hear the mewing cry of a buzzard overhead. Stately beech and birch trees overhang the path.

Walk downhill to reach a high bridge over the railway. This is a busy line and you will undoubtedly hear trains even if you don't see them. Continue through more mature woodland, a lovely walk generally descending gently to join another path beside the Allan Water, which burbles and sings over the rocks.

Pass between two grand old beech trees and reach the bridge over the river. Cross and turn left, briefly retracing the outward route to the triple signpost. Turn right here (Dunblane via Glen Road) and follow a stony track uphill through the trees. The path soon levels out and becomes more grassy, with views to the right.

Reach the access road to Drumdruills and continue downhill. Meet a minor road and turn left. You may see a llama in a field on the left. Continue on the road, which is now closed to traffic due to erosion. Past a barrier, it becomes a narrower path as it swings right into Kippenrait Glen. The glen is designated as an SSSI (Site of Special Scientific interest) due to its rich botanical interest and ancient woodland.

Before long you pass two landslips (the reason for the road closure). The slope to the left is steep and unstable, and pressure from water or frost can easily lead to erosion of this kind. The woodland becomes very dense and dark for a time as the path leads to the old Wharry Bridge, a lovely high stone arch built in the early 19th century.

Climb out of the glen to the point where the road is once again open to traffic. The road is now less enclosed, with expanding views as you approach the Kippenross turn. Over to the left is Pisgah Wood. The curious name comes from the Bible — Pisgah was the hill where Moses stood and viewed the Promised Land.

Reach the junction with the Sheriffmuir Road and continue. Join the pavement and pass Gamekeeper's Cottage, actually a substantial house, and then Pisgah Farm. The road runs down past many fine detached houses to the Fourways Roundabout.

Cross the road at the roundabout and walk down into the town, turning left for the station or right for the cathedral.

ASHFIELD AND KINBUCK

Distance	9km (5.5 miles) circular.
Start and finish	The Haining car park, Dunblane (behind the Cathedral).
Terrain	Road, tracks and good paths. Boots only needed in wet conditions.
Map	Free Dunblane path leaflet available locally.
Public transport	Dunblane Station is a short walk from the start.
Refreshments	Good choice in Dunblane.
Opening hours	**Dunblane Cathedral** (Historic Scotland) is open Apr-Sep Mon-Sat 9.30am-6pm, Sun 2pm-6pm; Oct-Mar Mon-Sat 9.30am-4.30pm, Sun 2pm-4.30pm. Admission is free. Further information from *www.historicscotland.gov.uk* or *www.dunblanecathedral.org.uk* The **Cathedral Museum**, in the 1624 Dean's House, is free and is well worth a visit.
Further information	If you visit *www.dunblaneweb.co.uk* you can find out much more about the town and the area. You can also pick up an excellent Historic Town Trail leaflet locally. There is a seasonal Tourist Information Centre (open April-October) near the station.

This easy walk links Dunblane with two attractive villages and provides an opportunity to visit a wonderful historic church.

From the car park, walk past Leighton House and turn left on Braeport. Continue uphill into Ramoyle. This was once the main route into Dunblane from the north. Ramoyle was a settlement of handloom weavers, and some of the houses date back to the 18th century.

Look for an old stone notice on a house wall saying 'Laighhill Loan 1888'. Turn left here and continue down the path to the Scouring Burn, another indication that cloth was worked in the area. Turn right immediately after crossing the burn and then recross it. Climb steps and fork left.

This is a lovely grassy path with lots of wild flowers in spring and summer. There are rowan trees and wild rose bushes too. Go through a wooden gate, and continue with the path. Walk through a wood by a wall and reach the cemetery access road. Recross the burn, and take the path to the right of the cemetery wall.

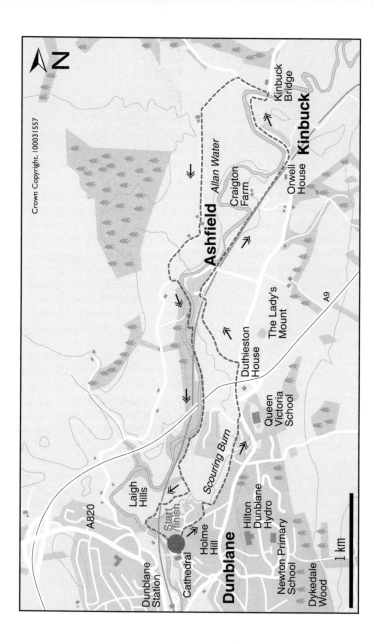

The old street of Ramoyle in Dunblane

Reach a road (Bellenden Grove) and go left of the roundabout, following signs for Perth and Kinbuck to cross the A9. As you do so you will see the Braes of Doune windfarm up to the left. This is a major development which will eventually hold 50 wind turbines and will dominate the skyline. I leave it to you to decide if this is a good thing or not.

Opposite the slip road for Perth, go left through a gate into a large field (signpost for Ashfield). Ignore the direction of the sign. Follow the track inside the gate for about 100 metres, then go half-right aiming towards the new house you can see (and the windfarm). You should pick up a path going over a low rise. This path steadily improves as it heads towards the railway line.

At the fence it meets a better path. Turn right and walk along by the fence until you reach the bridge over the railway. If you arrive there by a slightly different route, it doesn't really matter! The railway is the main line to Perth, Aberdeen and Inverness, and this section was opened in 1845.

Once over the bridge, turn right into Ashfield. This is another former weaving settlement with attractive rows of former weavers' cottages. Pass the bus shelter and continue on the path, signed for Kinbuck, beside the

WALK 5

19

railway with the Allan Water chuckling along on your left. At a gate go through and continue along field edges to Craigton farm. The next section can flood in winter. If this appears to be the case, use the farm access road under the railway and turn left on the road into Kinbuck.

If it is dry, continue with the path, eventually climbing onto the road and turning left. Kinbuck is another attractive village, and the road winds along beside the Allan Water round several bends to reach Kinbuck Bridge.

Cross the bridge and immediately turn left on a minor road. At a fork, keep left. The right fork goes into the Cromlix Estate, where Cromlix House is a high-class country house hotel renowned for its food.

Continue with the road for about a kilometre past Waterside and Hutchison until, at a sharp right bend, there is a signpost pointing left into a field. Go through the gate and walk down the side of the field. Continue round the bottom of the field, and at its far corner go through a small gate and take the path behind the house, which runs down to a footbridge over the river.

Cross the bridge. The scene here is very pretty with the water rushing through and trees overhanging the bank. There's even a small beach — ideal for picnics!

Once across the bridge, go right on a path by the river. It joins another path and then heads down steps, path and river passing under the railway together. Continue along the edge of a field. Pass under the A9 on a purpose-built path and continue beside the river for a time.

The path then leaves the river, with a railway bridge below, and reaches new houses. Take the rather uncomfortable stony path past the houses and then go steeply downhill to the railway before swinging left into the area known as the Laigh (low) Hills. At the top of the rise you get a good view of Gargunnock Crags.

Take the first main path on the right (before the houses) and keep right past tyres in the ground marking a cycle track. Continue with this main path to cross the railway. Once across, turn immediately left and follow the path down to a play area.

Turn left to rejoin the Allan Water. Go under the railway and keep left up to the car park. A visit to Dunblane Cathedral rounds off the walk nicely. This wonderful old building dates back in part to the 13th century, and still serves the town today. It is now in the care of Historic Scotland.

Dunblane Cathedral

The church is dedicated to St Blane after whom the town is also named (the dun, or fort, of Blane). He was a 6th-century Irish missionary who founded a number of churches in this part of Scotland. The Cathedral is on the site of one of Blane's original churches, so has a religious history going back nearly 1500 years.

WALK 5

21

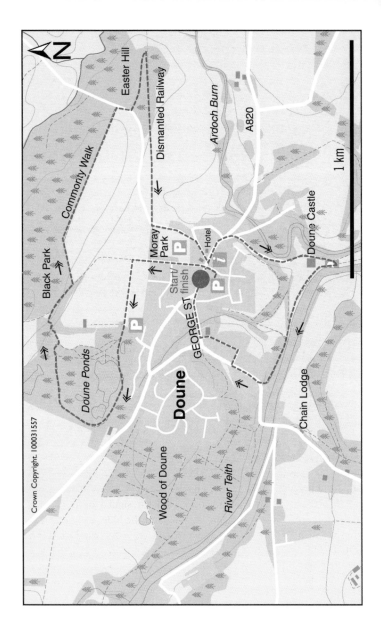

AROUND DOUNE

Distance	5km (3.5 miles) circular.
Start and finish	Castlehill car park, Doune.
Terrain	Road, tracks and good paths. Boots only needed in wet conditions.
Map	Free Doune and Deanston path leaflet available locally.
Public transport	Reasonable bus service from Dunblane to Doune.
Refreshments	Reasonable choice in Doune.
Opening hours	**Doune Castle** (Historic Scotland) is open Apr-Sep daily 9.30am-6pm,; Oct daily 9.30am-4.30pm; Nov-Mar Sat-Wed 9.30am-4pm. Admission charge. Further information from www.historicscotland.gov.uk.
Further information:	You can find out more about the village at the **Kilmadock Heritage and Information Centre** near the start. Open Mon-Sat 10am-4pm, Sun 2pm-4pm. Tel: 01786 841250. There is a website at *www.douneanddeanston.net*.

This short but varied and pleasant walk explores the countryside around Doune and also visits a superb castle.

From the car park, return to the main street at the Heritage Centre (run by volunteers and well worth a visit if open) and cross into Moray Street, passing the parish church. You will notice that the parish is Kilmadock rather than Doune. The name comes from the early missionary St Madoc.

Continue up Moray Street, passing the toilets, with Moray Park on the right. Cross the old railway line and then turn left on the access road for Doune Ponds. Continue along this road to the car park, where there is an information board and leaflet box. In the car park is a standing stone known locally as the Deil's Heid.

Take the path from the car park and fork left, signed for the viewing hide. You soon come to the largest pond and the hide. Doune Ponds, on the site of an old sand and gravel quarry, are still owned by Moray Estates but have been managed by Stirling Council since 1983 as a nature reserve. There is a good variety of waterfowl, and the woodland includes stands of birch and willow. In spring the woods are rich with bluebells.

Continue with the path, an attractive walk through the trees, and pass the hide for the second, smaller pond. You then turn right through the wood on a rather vague path. Cross a gully by a footbridge and reach a more defined path that winds pleasantly through the trees. The third (North) pond is hidden away to the left.

If you have picked up the leaflet, you can follow the nature trail using the numbered posts to get more detailed information. At a junction with a seat go ahead, not right, and reach post no 8.

Here you leave the nature trail, which goes to the right, and keep ahead on a clear path, soon climbing a series of steps around zig-zags to reach a vehicle track. Turn right on the track. A seat on the right gives a good view of the village with the Gargunnock Hills beyond.

Follow the track down and at the edge of the wood turn left as signed for the Commonty Path. Follow this lovely path as it climbs along the edge of the wood. 'Commonty' refers to the common grazings used in the past by villagers for their domestic beasts. Cattle and sheep would be grazed outside the village before being herded in at night. This ceased when the 1897 Public Health Act decreed that it was unhealthy to keep animals in byres attached to (or in some cases part of) dwelling houses.

The area to the left of the path, now forested, would have been open grazing land at one time. Note on the right a fine row of old beeches, possibly once a dense hedge. A seat gives another good view, with Dumyat over to the left.

The path levels out with mature conifers to the left, then passes a dense young plantation which includes beech and oak trees. The path eventually runs gently down to meet the Argaty road. Turn right and in 100 metres go left as signed on a broad, firm track through tall conifers.

This track runs easily down to meet the former Stirling to Callander and Oban railway line, now part of National Cycle Route 76. Turn right and follow the old line along. This was a wonderfully scenic route which closed in the 1960s, partly as a result of general cutbacks and partly through a major landslip in Glen Ogle, further north.

It now makes for a very straight, level path, with seats along the way if you need a rest. In time you pass over the Argaty road and then immediately turn left into Moray Park. Walk down the side of the park,

Doune Castle

through the car park and join the road. At the main road opposite the Heritage Centre, turn left.

In about 250 metres turn right on the access road to Doune Castle and follow the signs. The castle would once have been the focal point for the village, with small dwellings clustered around it. It is strategically placed at the confluence of the Teith and Ardoch rivers, on the edge of the Highlands. Much of it is 14th century, and it was a stronghold of the Dukes of Albany. It is notable for having relatively few later additions. In the 15th and 16th centuries it was regularly used as a royal hunting lodge.

In more recent times the castle saw 'battle' of a rather different kind when it was used as one of the locations for the film *Monty Python and the Holy Grail*. Not quite what the original builders had in mind, perhaps!

To return to the village, follow the exit road from the car park and turn left as signed through a metal gate. Turn right through the wood to a gate, then follow the field edge to another gate. Walk up the road a short distance and swing round to the left. At the crossroads, turn right and the car park is 100 metres along on the left.

WALK 6

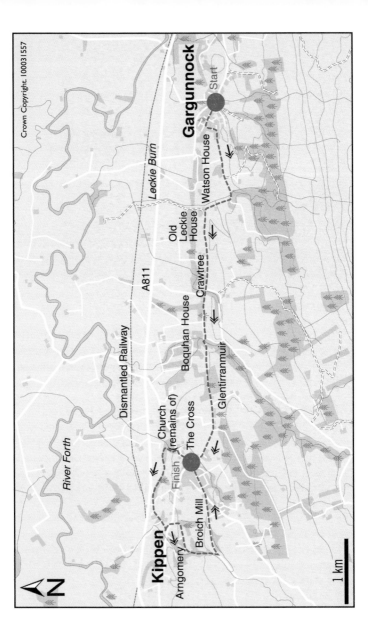

GARGUNNOCK AND KIPPEN

Distance	7km (4 miles) linear plus 4km (2.5 miles) circular. Total 11km (6.5 miles).
Start	Bus stop in Leckie Road, Gargunnock. Park tidily in Kippen and take the bus to Gargunnock (hourly Mon-Sat, two-hourly Sun).
Finish	The Cross, Kippen.
Terrain	Road, tracks and generally good paths. Boots only needed in wet conditions.
Map	Free Gargunnock and Kippen path leaflets available locally.
Public transport	Regular buses from Stirling to both villages.
Refreshments	Inn in Gargunnock. Two inns and a deli/café in Kippen.
Toilets	None on the route.
Further information	If you visit www.gargunnock.org.uk you can find out much more about the village and the area. The nearest Tourist Information Centre (open all year) is in Stirling.

These two attractive villages west of Stirling both have good path systems. A beautiful walk links them, and you can extend your day (perhaps after a break for refreshments) by a pleasant circuit from Kippen.

From the bus stop in Gargunnock, walk down to the church and go up the steps below the bell tower. There is a lovely view looking north to the hills from here and a view indicator has been provided.

Return the way you came and take the left fork (Main Street) past the Gargunnock Inn. In the 19th century the village was a centre for basket weaving and had a grain mill. Gargunnock House was owned by Captain James Stirling, whose ship HMS *Ferret* accompanied Napoleon into exile on St Helena. His daughter Jane was a very talented pianist and in the 1830s is said to have received lessons from Chopin, who may have visited Gargunnock.

In the 1930s it was said that this street 'led to nowhere', but in your case this certainly isn't true. Continue up the hill and near the top, turn left into Drummond Place. Just before no 20, turn right on a path known as the Beeches. At first the trees are more birches, but

The old straight road between Gargunnock and Kippen

there are some fine old beeches later on. There is a good view looking left to Gargunnock Crags.

At the end of the path join a road and continue ahead. Pass a sign for Knock-o-Ronald Farm, with Watson House, a classical 1820s mansion, over to the right. Cross the Leckie Burn and turn right (at a shed) on a track running beside the burn. At a junction with a signpost, turn left.

You are now on the old military road (now just a track), built by soldiers in the late 18th century to link the castles at Dumbarton and Stirling. It was part of a substantial network of new roads constructed to ease communications for the army in the wake of the Jacobite uprisings. The 17th-century Old Leckie House may be glimpsed on the right. All of this area is in the Leckie Estate, long associated with the Younger family of brewing fame.

As you follow the line of the old road there are superb views to the right towards Ben Ledi, Ben Venue and further west towards Ben Lomond. The track is very straight. Pass Crawtree and continue to the road at Burntown of Boquhan. Cross a burn and pass a long red sandstone building, originally a school. The datestone says 'Kirkton of Boquhan rebuilt AD 1798'.

Where the road bends right, go ahead between stone pillars. The track becomes grassy. Go through a gate at a barn. Further on, to the right is Boquhan House with its beautifully manicured grounds, dotted with fine trees. Cross the old Bridge of Boquhan and go through a gate into an open field. Take the right fork. There are usually cattle here so please keep dogs on a lead.

Near the end of the field, up on the left, is a small dun or fort called Broken Castle. Go through a kissing gate into Trough Wood, on a narrow path between rhododendrons. You are still on the line of the old military road.

Reach a road. A large house on the right has a 2003 datestone; it is good to see this tradition being maintained. The road goes steadily uphill to Glentirranmuir. At the second junction (signpost) turn left and in 100 metres go right (signpost) into Burnside Wood on a track. At a fork, keep left on a path that winds through the wood.

Follow the path to a sports field. Cross the field to the exit (signpost) and turn right on a rough road. Follow this road across a burn, where it improves, then go right into Castlehill Loan. Follow this road round to the left and into Main Street, Kippen. The pub, café and cross are all down to the right.

Kippen Pond

Kippen is a lovely village and has a long history. There were weavers here, and at one time a large vineyard flourished. There was even, believe it or not, a thriving boatbuilder — and there is still a clockmaker, William Dougall. His ancestors made the church clock in 1881. Much of the area's business has always been agricultural and a ploughing society was established as early as 1835. There are many fine walks in the area, one of which is sampled here.

From the old cross (also the war memorial) walk down the cobbled Rennie's Lane. The Smiddy was given to the National Trust for Scotland in 1982 by Andrew Rennie, sixth-generation blacksmith here. Behind it was the old parish church, built in the 17th century. Little remains. The present church with its distinctive square bell tower dates from 1825.

Continue down a path behind houses, passing a particularly lovely garden with a view of the church tower. Briefly join a road and continue ahead with a big view to the right.

Pass white gateposts and continue down the path. At a roadway near the A811, turn left. Pass farm buildings, go through metal gates and at a junction turn left (there is a pavement). The view to the left now includes the Braes of Doune windfarm.

Take the next entry on the right (signpost) through gateposts and follow the access road to Arngomery House. Before the house, fork left up to a gate leading into a field.

Follow the edge of the field (there may be cattle here) to reach a small gate leading into woodland with the Broich Burn below to the right. Follow the delightful wee path through the wood. There are many old trees and the ground cover includes ramsons (wild garlic).

Reach a road at Broich Mill. Its datestone records that it was built in 1801 and rebuilt 1929 by R.L. Ewing. It is in a beautiful setting.

Follow the access road out, and at a junction turn left. The rest of the walk is on tarmac but there are fine views across the low-lying carse land to the hills as compensation.

Pass a house with a lovely park-like garden and reach the outskirts of Kippen. In time you join the Fintry road and walk back down Main Street. On the right is the Coronation Garden, a play area set up in 1953, and on the left is the primary school, which has links with Kikambala school in faraway Kenya. The contrast between the douce village here in Scotland and the small township in Africa could hardly be more extreme.

DUMYAT

Distance	9km (5.5 miles) circular.
Ascent	450 metres approx.
Start and Finish	Cocksburn Wood car park (GR815987). To get there, take the A9 from Stirling to Bridge of Allan. Pass the main entrance to the University of Stirling and take the next right (Kenilworth Road). Take the first right, signed for Sheriffmuir. Follow this road up for 2.5km to reach the car park on the left (in old pines, close to a large electricity pylon).
Terrain	Good tracks and hill paths. Boots recommended.
Map	Harveys Ochil Hills 1:25,000 walkers map.
Public transport	None to the start.
Refreshments	None on route. Nearest in Bridge of Allan.
Toilets	None on route.

Dumyat, at the western end of the Ochils, is a popular little hill, and rightly so. It is splendidly craggy and gives excellent views. The hill is often climbed from Blairlogie on the A91, but the ascent from there is brutally steep. I prefer the approach from the Sheriffmuir Road, which apart from providing good views from the outset, starts from nearly 200m up and thus offers a more gradual climb.

Let's clarify the name first. Although only 6 letters, it is split into 3 syllables and is pronounced 'Dum-eye-at' not 'Dum-yat' as might seem more obvious.

The circuit described here gives a satisfying walk. It does mean there is an inevitable 2km of road walking, but by parking at Cocksburn Wood you can split this in two. Leave the car park and walk back down the road. To the right is a lovely view over Cocksburn Reservoir towards the distant Ben Lomond.

In just under a kilometre, as the road bends sharp right, you reach an informal parking area. At the north end of this area, go through the upper metal gate onto a clear path and keep left at a fork.

As you start to climb, there is a view to the right of the Wallace Monument and Stirling. Dumyat itself is hidden. The view soon expands to include Gargunnock Crags, the Forth and the carse between. Stirling University campus is below you.

WALK 8

31

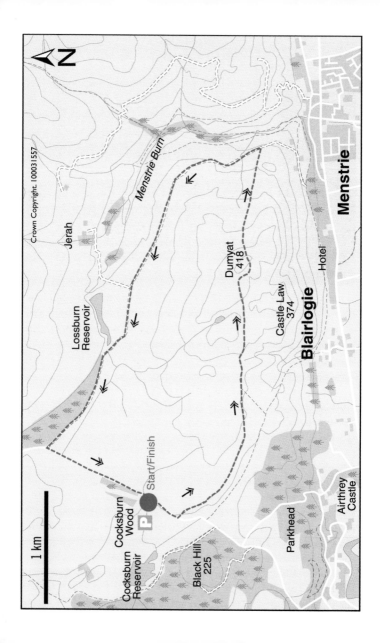

The approach to Dumyat

Dumyat soon appears, looking every inch a proper little mountain, which indeed it is. The vista of the Forth now stretches beyond Kincardine Bridge. Cross a small gully and climb round a shoulder, continuing the ascent with Dumyat looking ever nearer. There are several lovely little corners along here where you can take a break if you feel like it. You now have a big hill panorama behind and to the left.

Cross the foot of a scree slope. You then cross the upper part of the Warloch Glen. A warlock is a male witch, and there is a Witch's Craig not far away too. You can see the summit but the last section always seem to take longer than it should. Eventually you reach Dumyat's top at 418m.

There are various bits of hill 'furniture' including a large brazier, two plaques to men of the Argyll & Sutherland Highlanders and a representation of the regiment's badge in a rather depressing grey colour.

Ignore all these and concentrate on the view, which is superb. To the south is the carse, the Forth and Stirling. To the north are massed ranks of hills including Ben Ledi, Ben Vorlich, Stuc a'Chroin and many more. Eastward the Ochils show as waves of green, with Ben Cleuch just above the rest. The Hillfoots towns nestle at the foot of the scarp.

Dumyat is a volcanic plug of igneous rock, as also are Abbey Craig (Wallace Monument) and Castle Rock in Stirling. The steep scarp of the Ochils' south face looks from here like a fault line, but in fact it

WALK 8

33

isn't. It is just a major geological uplift. The nature of the rock means that the ground is fertile, hence the long tradition of agriculture here, and also the wide range of wild flowers seen in spring and summer.

When you are ready to leave, go down a small gully left of the summit to pick up a path which goes fairly directly down the hill to the east, so that you lose height rapidly. This is a way up Dumyat from Menstrie.

Before long the gradient eases and the path improves. Follow it down with a small burn on the left. At a fork go left down to a clear junction, and turn left here.

This is the start of a lovely traverse round the back of Dumyat, on generally unfrequented paths in beautiful surroundings. Menstrie Glen is below you. There is an initial steady climb, but after that the path is reasonably level and you can stride out. There are several wet patches but all can be avoided. Grouse are found on these moors and you may well hear their distinctive rattling call.

As the path swings left, you see ahead across the glen the former inbye land of the long abandoned hill farm of Jerah. A long, gentle climb leads to a junction. Keep left, now on a track, and descend to pass the end of the small Lossburn Reservoir, almost hidden in a fold in the hills.

Go through a gate and continue with the track beside a plantation. Dumyat is now over your left shoulder. A brisk 15-minute walk, mostly gently uphill and probably against the wind as you are walking west, leads up to the road. Turn left and wander along the final kilometre back to the car park, reflecting as you do so on the pleasures of the walk you have just enjoyed.

Lossburn Reservoir, almost hidden in the hills

BEN CLEUCH

Distance	12km (7.5 miles) circular.
Ascent	650 metres approx.
Start and Finish	Wood Hill Woodland Park car park. The park is signed from just east of Alva on the A91. Follow the road up the hill and park as directed.
Terrain	Good tracks and hill paths. Boots essential. Take waterproofs and windproofs, map and compass and some food and drink.
Map	Harveys Ochil Hills 1:25,000 walkers map or OS Landranger sheet 58 (Perth & Alloa).
Public transport	None to the start. Good bus service from Stirling to Alva and Tillicoultry.
Refreshments	None on route. Nearest in Alva and Tillicoultry.
Toilets	None on route. Nearest in Alva and Tillicoultry.

Ben Cleuch is the highest point in the Ochils, at 721m, and is worth climbing for that reason alone. It is not a dramatic peak but does command excellent views and its ascent gives a satisfying half-day walk.

From the car park, cross the road and take the signed path slanting left up the hill through the trees. This area is owned by the Woodland Trust and carefully managed to ensure maximum regeneration of the native species.

The path ascends steadily, then flattens out to cross the Silver Burn by a small footbridge. The name reflects the fact that a vein of silver was indeed found here, and the precious metal extracted, during the 18th century. The mine was set up by Sir John Erskine of Alva House (1672-1739), a man of quick temper of whom it was said that he was 'of more wit than wisdom'. At one time the silver was realising £4,000 a week, a huge amount for the time. All traces have long gone.

Reach the open hill and continue climbing on the vehicle track which twists round several bends as it gains height, eventually reaching a gate where the gradient eases. The Nebit is to the left and Wood Hill to the right. Looking back, the view has expanded to take in the winding Forth and the plain below.

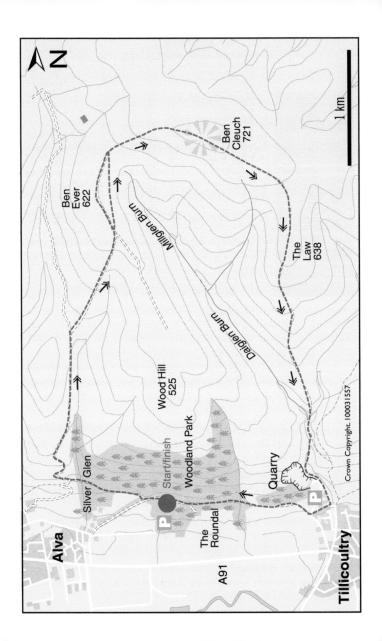

N

Alva

Silver Glen

Ben Ever
622

Ben Cleuch
721

Start/finish

Woodland Park

Wood Hill
525

Milglen Burn

The Roundal

The Law
638

Daiglen Burn

Quarry

A91

Tillicoultry

Crown Copyright. 100031557

1 km

Ben Cleuch from Ben Ever

Continue with the track for about another 700m to a point where a short spur joins from the right. You leave the track here and face a stiff climb on a grassy path up the obvious slope ahead, on to Ben Ever. This section is unrelenting so take your time and stop when you want, to enjoy the views.

At the top of the section, by a small pond, go left. You now have the choice of going over Ben Ever or round it. Either way there is a reasonable path, and the two routes join on the far side of the hill. You can see Ben Cleuch to the right.

Cross the stile and go right, by the fence, up another steady climb on to Ben Cleuch which rises steeply above you. The path is quite clear. Partway up it leaves the fence and heads to the right. The slope eases and you can see your summit ahead. The last section is straightforward and then you reach the top of Ben Cleuch, which has a stone wind shelter and the remains of an old view indicator.

The panorama is pretty good. To the east, north and west the green Ochils roll away. Further north are the higher hills of the Southern Highlands, while to the south you look over the plain of the Forth and far beyond. Edinburgh is usually quite visible, and you may even see right out to North Berwick Law in very clear conditions. It's worth the effort to enjoy all this.

WALK 9

37

When you are ready to leave, take the obvious path near the fence, heading south. The path sticks close to the fence, with one leftward kink, as it descends gently over ground which can often be boggy. The path then curves right and a short climb leads you to the Law (638m).

From here, Tillicoultry seems almost at your feet, and the southward view is excellent. The descent that follows is very direct, and has one or two slightly tricky sections. The path shoots straight down the hill, and it is worth taking time over it as it is quite eroded in places.

Your descent is rapid and before long you are nearing the glen. The last section is the trickiest — a short (5m) scramble down a badly eroded section, but if you take it steadily it should not pose any great difficulty. At the foot of this section you cross the burn and then go up to reach the glen path. Keep right.

The walk down Mill Glen is lovely, crossing and recrossing the burn several times among the trees with the rushing water always close by. The final section leads you past the massive Tillicoultry Quarry, which has eaten deeply into the hill.

Reach the road and walk down by the burn for a short way until you see a sign on the right saying 'Alva 1½'. It's actually a bit further than that, but you aren't going all the way to Alva so it doesn't really matter! Follow the sign across the burn and along a short road to its end. A little path then leads through a scrubby piece of ground to emerge on a wide vehicle track that serves the quarry.

Turn right and then take the left fork on a track leading across the hill, with the golf course to your left. This track leads easily up into the woodland for the final section of the walk. This is a lovely walk through mature trees.

As you approach the car park you pass the stable block of the former Alva House. This was a classical 17th-century mansion built for the Erskines, and greatly extended during the 19th century. After lying disused for some time it met an undignified end when used as an artillery target for training during World War Two. The stables date from the early 19th century. They were used as a hotel (called the Farriers) for a while but at the time of writing were again a private house.

It is now just a short step back to the car park.

ACROSS THE OCHILS

Distance	14.5km (9 miles) linear.
Start	Tillicoultry.
Finish	Blackford.
Terrain	Tracks and mostly good paths. Some unpathed sections and wet or boggy stretches. Boots essential. Take a map and compass, good waterproofs and windproofs, and sufficient food and drink with you.
Map	Harveys Ochil Hills walkers map or OS Landranger sheet 58.
Public transport	See note below.
Refreshments	Good choice in Tillicoultry. Reasonable choice in Blackford.
Toilets	In Tillicoultry or Blackford. None on the route.
Note	It is quite easy to do this walk using public transport, using Stirling as the point of a triangle. There are frequent buses from Stirling to Tillicoultry, and a reasonable service from Blackford back to Stirling. You could of course use two cars, but using the buses is a 'greener' way of doing the walk and also more fun.

This superb walk follows the longest and highest of the old through routes across the Ochil Hills. At least, it attempts to, as part of the original line of the right of way has been lost under Glendevon Reservoir. This entails a longish diversion over sometimes pathless, often boggy ground where a little perseverance may be necessary. The highest section of the walk also needs some care, and the walk is not recommended for inexperienced walkers in poor conditions or mist. Having said that, on a good day it is a fine expedition which provides a variety of terrain and excellent views.

The walk proper starts at the foot of Mill Glen in Tillicoultry, reached by walking up Upper Mill Road from the A91. At the small car park here, you will see a right of way sign to Blackford. Follow the sign and almost immediately go left (yellow arrow) up a long flight of steps and through a gate onto the hill.

The route now follows a series of zig-zags which typify a classic hill path. Keep to the main path and don't be tempted by the steeper

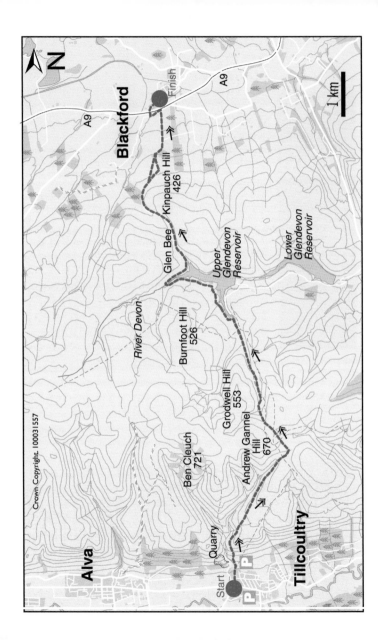

shortcuts; using these will only cause erosion. You soon get a wide view back across Tillicoultry to the plain of the Forth.

There are further steps, which finally end at a point with a seat just up to the right (broken at the time of writing). The route you need goes up behind this seat and soon resumes its zig-zag progress before climbing more steadily round the hill. Keeping below the seat here will lead you to a path back down into the glen.

The path contours purposefully around the hill, above the Gannel Burn. At about GR917987 you reach gateposts. Take the path to the left here, not the route along the fence to the right. The views are now extensive and there is a great feeling of space. The path begins to level out, meandering delightfully along the hillside before reaching the head of the Gannel Burn.

Turn left across a boggy area and continue along a smaller path following the fenceline. This is an important point – don't be tempted by the larger path which forks off left and leads up to Andrew Gannel Hill. Stay with the fence until you approach the col, where a fence junction and an old metal stile indicate the walk's highest point at almost 600m. There are fine views all around and you can see the reservoir ahead and below.

Cross the stile and follow the path northwards as it skirts around Skythorn Hill (the fork to the right goes to the summit, a short and

Russet and gold in the Ochils

easy diversion if you want to bag the hill). The right of way continues along an obvious path, descending steadily along a broad grassy ridge. Continue to the 450m col at GR219026. There is another important waypoint here. Don't take the clear vehicle tracks leading up to the right onto the higher ground; instead, take the much smaller path which branches off to the left. Although narrow, this path is quite clear, contouring easily along the hillside above the Broich Burn.

Meet a bigger path which is then followed left, downhill and along to the bridge over the Broich Burn. Cross the bridge ('Path to Black-ford' sign), and up the track to where another sign directs you to the right. A very indistinct path leads across a field heading for a stile over the next fence. Cross a small burn, after which the path becomes more obvious. It is a very attractive scene looking across the reservoir to the hill slopes beyond.

Another stile leads to a descent to a small burn crossing, then go steeply up the bank to a stile. An encouraging yellow arrow points WNW. Follow a faint path in the general direction indicated by the arrow to a gate at GR909041. You may see hares in this area.

Vehicle paths heading NNW become a small footpath before van-ishing into a peaty bog which makes for slow going. Try to keep rough-ly parallel to the shoreline. A better path does eventually appear, and this can then be followed to the bridge over the River Devon. Be sure to take the right fork after crossing the burn at GR903046.

Cross the bridge and follow the river back down towards the reservoir. The Devon, which rises south-west of here, flows through several reser-voirs before finally making its way down to the Forth. The scene ahead is lovely, especially in sunshine when the water is a bright blue. From au-tumn to spring you should see good numbers of Canada geese here.

The path turns away from the reservoir up little Glen Bee, crossing a stile and a ladder over a high fence in quick succession before continu-ing up the east side of the glen to meet a track leading up to a gate.

After this, you are on good tracks and there are no further difficul-ties. Cross the stile at the gate and take the left fork, heading down Kinpauch Glen (the right fork leads up on to Kinpauch Hill). There is another very wide view ahead across lower ground with the twin Munro summits of Ben Vorlich (the pointy one) and Stuc a'Chroin on the distant skyline.

Upper Glendevon Reservoir

The track continues downhill past a sizeable plantation with further good views and Blackford now clear ahead. Swing right and left and then turn right. On the left is the site of the long abandoned farmstead of Kinpauch. A grassy shortcut leads left, across to a small building — or you can just stay on the track.

You may see Highland Spring vehicles on this section as the company use water from the Ochils for their well-known bottled product, which is produced in Blackford. This should be an encouragement if you have drunk any burn water during the walk!

Walk out across the fields, over the Braes of Ogilvie, to reach a minor road next to the A9. If you are using two cars, this is the place to leave one of them. If you are using the bus, go left along the road, cross the A9 with extreme care — it is a very fast and busy dual carriageway — and walk into Blackford, where refreshments can be obtained at the visitor centre (if open) or an inn while you wait for the bus back to Stirling.

These old rights of way were once well used with plenty of foot and horse traffic, and it is important that we keep them open. Although this is a longish walk, I felt it was well worth including in the book, and I am sure you will agree that it makes a very satisfying and interesting day.

WALK 10

43

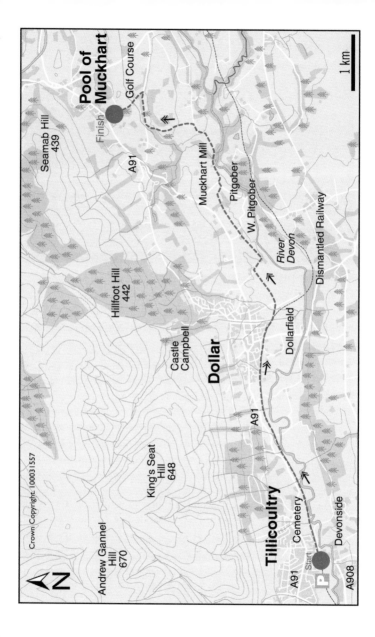

ALONG THE HILLFOOTS

Distance	10.5km (6.5 miles) linear.
Start	Moss Road car park, Tillicoultry. From the A91 turn down the A908 Alloa road (this is Moss Road) and in 400m the car park (unsigned) is on the right opposite the Devonvale Hall.
Finish	Pool of Muckhart. Return by bus.
Terrain	Road, tracks and good paths. Boots only needed in wet conditions.
Map	Harveys Ochil Hills walkers map plus OS Landranger sheet 58.
Public transport	Hourly bus Mon-Sat from Pool of Muckhart to Tillicoultry: less frequent on Sundays.
Refreshments	Good choice in Tillicoultry. Inn and coffee shop in Pool of Muckhart.
Toilets	In Tillicoultry. None on the route.

This easy low-level walk links several Hillfoots towns and villages and provides excellent views of the Ochils as well as good historical interest.

From the car park, cross the A908 and pick up the path, passing a Devon Way information board. To the left is Devonvale Hall, the date-stone displaying the butterfly symbol of Samuel Jones & Co, part of whose Devonvale paper mill (built 1860) is now the Sterling furniture warehouse.

Continue along the old railway line. Opened in 1867, it closed to passenger traffic, like so many of its kind, in the 1960s. Keep to the left-hand path (don't go through the gate). In spring and summer there are plenty of wild flowers and the trees which shade the path include rowans and elders.

The Devon pursues a convoluted course to your right and is only occasionally close to the path. Pass a neat double seat in memory of Angela Valente, cross a farm road and pass under a bridge. In summer the hill views to the left are obscured by the trees but in winter they are clearer.

Soon approach the outskirts of Dollar, joining a broad track which veers right, down to a sewage works. Keep with the path, passing under two bridges to reach the old platform for Dollar Station. It must have been a very pleasant ride along this line.

In a further 200 metres, at a junction, turn right and in 100m, go left on a track. You have left the railway, and can see the piers of its former bridge across the Devon to the right. You soon get a superb view up past Castle Campbell into the hills.

Follow the path as it winds through open countryside to reach West Pitgober ('place of goats'). Turn right on a lane, up to Linnbank Farm. Turn left here (signpost), through a gate into a field. Note the round building, an old 'gin mill' where a horse would once have walked round and round providing motive power.

There is a big hill view to the left. Go through a gate onto a path be-tween fences. Reach the houses at Pitgober and turn right on the road past attractive cottages. As the road dips and bends right, go left on a sunken path. It can be quite dark here, but it soon opens out. There are fine mature beech and birch trees.

Cross a stile and go over a small burn. Halfway across the next field the path swings right (no sign), normally keeping to the edge of the grass with a root crop on the left. It soon becomes clearer and runs up to a minor road. Turn left.

The water-wheel at Muckhart Mill

At the junction go right (footpath sign for Rumbling Bridge), and walk down the access road for Muckhart Mill. The mill dates back to 1666 but the main buildings, a very attractive group, are late 18th century. At over 6m diameter, the old water-wheel is one of the largest in Scotland. Note the fine sculpture of a horse in the garden. The mill is on the Hole Burn; the old bridge you crossed just before it has a masonic eye carving, supposed to ward off evil spirits.

Turn left on the track round an S-bend, passing a huge and long-disused lime kiln with three arched openings. Continue across fields, beginning the only uphill section of the walk as you swing left through a woodland strip with big old beeches. Curve right out of the wood and in 150m turn left (footpath sign).

Cross the shoulder of Fire Hill and follow the track round to the right and down through woods to a road. Turn right, and follow the road for about 500m to the entry to Muckhart Golf Club.

Turn left here, past the clubhouse, and then down to follow a rough track back up through a wood. Reach a road at Drumburn Farm, which has an impressive carving of an osprey on its gate. Continue along the road into Pool of Muckhart, with Seamab Hill rising beyond the houses.

At the Coronation Hall, turn right. The coronation of its name was that of King George V in 1911, and the hall was moved here from Glasgow. It has been restored with a Heritage Lottery grant. Turn right into the village centre. Pool of Muckhart has several times won the title of Best Kept Village in Scotland, and it is easy to see why. There are many attractive buildings, and in summer lovely flower displays and hanging baskets.

The inn and coffee shop both offer excellent hospitality, and either would be a good place to relax while waiting for the bus back to Tillicoultry. On the way back to your car from the bus stop in Murray Square you pass Tillicoultry's handsome clock tower, presented by Provost Murray in 1930, and as you walk down Moss Road note the fine 1930s villas, designed by Arthur Bracewell to the plan of Sidney Platfoot, managing director of the paper firm, who wished to create a harmonious environment for his workers and managers in the town. It is fair to say that he succeeded.

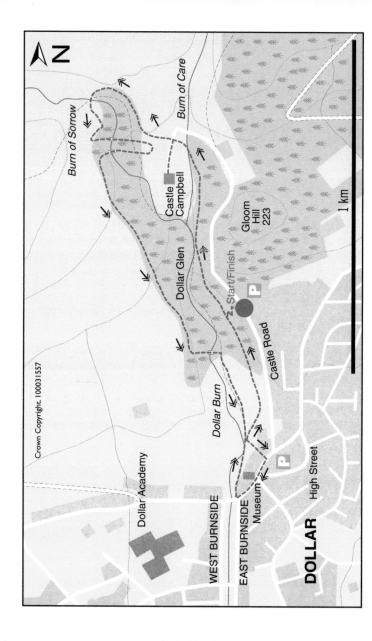

DOLLAR GLEN

Distance	5km (3 miles) circular.
Start and finish	Quarry car park, Dollar. Follow the signs for Castle Campbell from the A91 up East Burnside, Hillfoot Road and Castle Road. The last section is narrow and steep. The car park is about 500m up Castle Road on the right.
Terrain	Generally good paths. Some rough sections and also steep drops where care is needed, especially with children and dogs. Boots recommended.
Map	Harveys Ochil Hills walkers map.
Public transport	Regular bus service to Dollar from Stirling.
Refreshments	Good choice in Dollar. Seasonal coffee shop at the castle.
Toilets	In Dollar.
Opening hours	**Castle Campbell** is open 9.30-6.30 daily Apr-Oct, 9.30-4.30 daily Nov-Mar. Admission charge (free to HS and NTS members). For more information visit *www. historicscotland. gov.uk.* **Dollar Museum** is open at weekends only, Easter-Christmas.

This short but very enjoyable walk explores the spectacular Dollar Glen and also visits a magnificent castle and a very good local museum, so has plenty of interest.

From the car park, cross the road and take the path, winding down steps and round several bends to reach the main glen path. Turn right and start climbing. Dollar Glen — a true gorge — was carved out by the coming together of the fast-flowing Burn of Care and Burn of Sorrow, which form Dollar Burn after they meet below the castle.

The glen has very steep sides, and because of its remarkable geological formations and also the wide range of plants, including many mosses which thrive in the damp conditions, is designated as a Site of Special Scientific Interest. It was presented to the National Trust for Scotland, along with Castle Campbell, in 1950. The Trust manages the glen but the castle is now in the care of Historic Scotland.

The path levels out, the burn almost hidden below you, then crosses the first of several long bridges. This one was rebuilt in 2002. Reach the point where the two upper burns meet and go left to a viewpoint for the dramatic narrow cleft in the rocks known as Windy Edge Pass. There used to be a path through here but in 1997 a serious rock fall made it too dangerous to keep open.

Return to the main path and continue upwards, crossing another long bridge and then crossing the burn. To the right and above are many small waterfalls, known as Hempy's Falls and the Craiginnan Falls.

Go up a long flight of zig-zagging stone steps to reach the access road for Castle Campbell and turn left for a visit. The Clan Campbell (headed by the Earls, later Dukes, of Argyll) are more associated with lands and strongholds further west, but they held sway here too for centuries. The castle is in a wonderfully powerful position, and as might be expected, commands a superb view which is enhanced if you climb to the top of the tower.

Originally known as Castle Glume or Gloom (from a Gaelic word meaning 'chasm'), the building came to the Campbells in the late 15th century and its name was then changed. The Campbells were in residence here until the castle was attacked and badly damaged in 1654 by Cromwellian troops under General Monck. The castle remained in Campbell hands until 1805 when it became part of the Harviestoun

Castle Campbell sits proud above Dollar Glen

estate, and in 1948 Mr Kerr of Harviestoun gave it, with the glen, to the National Trust for Scotland, on whose behalf it is now managed by Historic Scotland. The remains are substantial, and a tour is strongly recommended.

Leave the castle and take the second path on the left, going uphill. King's Seat Hill is above to the left. Pass a bench with a fine view of the castle. At a fork go right (the left-hand path leads to a viewpoint for Sauchie Falls), climb zigzags, go through a gate and continue with the small gorge of the Burn of Sorrow below.

Reach a footbridge, with a beautiful small waterfall to the right. Cross and turn left. There is a lot of natural woodland around here. Follow the path downhill. It is quite narrow and there are steep drops, so please take care. Go round zigzags and down a miniature gorge to a footbridge across the burn. Go up steps, at a fork go left and then (before the gate) go sharply back right down to the footbridge you can see below.

This leads to the newer path down the western side of the glen, built after the rock fall closed Windy Edge Pass. Climb initially to the edge of the gorge, then go through the gateway (not over the stile) and on to an easy downhill section, for part of the time with the golf course to your right.

Zigzags lead you back down to the gorge and a footbridge. Turn right and walk across Mill Green (once a bleaching green for cloth). A plaque records the opening in 1979, by HRH Princess Anne, of a refurbished path system.

At a fork go left up to the road, then right, round to Dollar Museum. Try to time your visit for its opening hours. The museum is run by volunteers and contains much of local and historical interest. Leave the museum and turn right, back on to Mill Green. Continue onto the glen path past the information board.

The path leads up to the turn-off for the car park in about 400m. This turn-off is not signed so watch carefully to ensure you don't miss it. As you climb back up you can reflect on all that you have seen — quite a lot for such a short walk, and well worth a return visit. Dollar Glen is very attractive at all times of the year. The autumn colouring is lovely, and in winter the lack of vegetation means you can see the gorge and the falls more clearly.

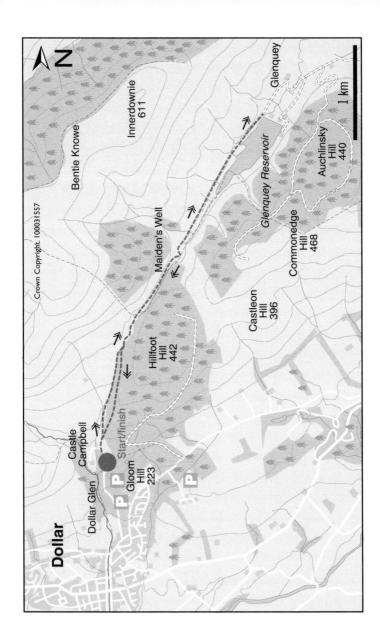

GLEN QUEY

Distance	8km (5 miles) circular.
Start and Finish	Upper car park, Dollar Glen. Note: If this car park (which only holds 16 cars) is full, you will need to use the main car park lower down, which will add 1km to the walk distance.
Terrain	Generally good tracks and paths. Some stretches can be muddy. Boots or strong shoes recommended.
Map	Harveys Ochil Hills walkers' map.
Public transport	Regular bus services from Stirling to Dollar.
Refreshments	Reasonable choice in Dollar.
Toilets	In Dollar. None on the route.

This easy low-level walk goes through an intriguing narrow pass and visits a beautiful reservoir. Try to pick a good day; in fine weather the surroundings are stunning. The route follows another old right of way through the hills, this one linking Dollar with Glen Devon.

From the car park, walk up the short section of road to the house, and at the fork, keep right, uphill (the left fork goes down to the glen and castle). The path rises steadily. There is a great view of King's Seat, up to the left, and before long Castle Campbell can be seen behind you, dominating the upper part of Dollar Glen.

Continue climbing with the Burn of Care below to the left. A wider view down to the Forth opens up behind you. At a forest gate, keep left outside the wood, which is a typical conifer plantation. Follow the path, which can be rather boggy, to a stile. There is a nice little water-fall down to the left.

Rejoin the forest track and follow it down across the burn. Immediately go right on the path climbing steeply up the bank, and continue along the top of the bank, again through some boggy sections. Whitewisp Hill towers up to the left. Continue with the path to another stile — rather a high, awkward step that needs a little care.

You then join a path emerging from the forest. This is part of the return route, so you might like to note where it goes off into the trees. The path then improves for much of the way as you approach the head of Glen Quey through a dramatic little pass which is increasingly constrained. There are small crags to the left and the dense trees climb up the hillside on the right. Go through a metal kissing gate with another small waterfall up to the left.

Continue with the path, picking your way across several small burns, none of which should prove difficult. The pass is quite an exciting place but can also be a wind tunnel.

In time, the forestry draws back on the right and the views start to open up. As you round a small hillock you have the Glen Quey Burn to the right, and get your first glimpse of the reservoir ahead.

Cross two stiles in quick succession, with a footbridge between them and another waterfall on the left. Then go through a high gate onto Woodland Trust ground. A notice explains that the Trust is planting this 380-hectare site with over 400,000 broad-leaved trees, including oak, birch and rowan. The scene will change quite dramatically in the decades ahead as these trees mature. The Trust also hopes to develop further walking routes here.

Continue, now on a firm grassy track, to reach the reservoir. Fringed with trees and surrounded by hills, it makes a truly beautiful scene. There are usually some water birds, and on the hills you can

Approaching Glenquey Reservoir

Glenquey Reservoir

hear the 'cronk' of ravens and possibly spot a grouse whirring by. The reservoir is stocked with trout and you may well see anglers trying their luck.

The track crosses the Meadow Burn and then the Blackrigg Burn to reach the dam impounding the reservoir. The walk stops here, but by using the map you could, if you wished, continue to Glendevon where you can get food and drink at the Tormaukin Inn. For now, relax and take in the lovely surroundings before starting to walk back.

Follow the path back up to the pass and make your way through. Once through the metal kissing gate, watch in about another 250 metres for the turnoff into the forest.

It is initially very dark in the trees and can feel quite eerie. Sections of the path can also be boggy, but it soon improves both in terms of getting lighter and with a better surface.

The path broadens and dries out, eventually joining a forest track which runs down to the gate you passed near the start of the walk.

Go through, admiring again the truly lovely view of King's Seat and Castle Campbell. From here it is a short downhill walk back to the car park. If you have time, you can easily visit Castle Campbell while you are here (details in Walk 12).

WALK 13

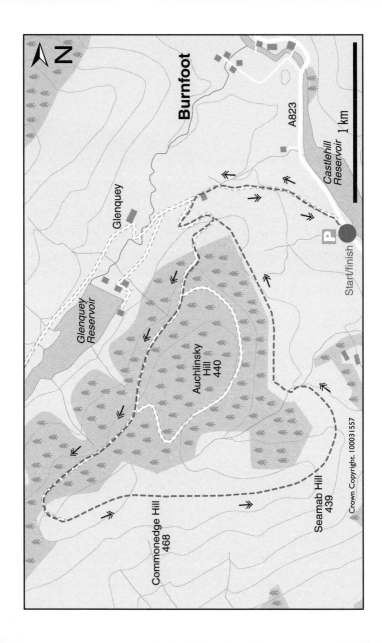

Burnfoot

Glenquey

Glenquey Reservoir

Auchlinsky Hill 440

Commonedge Hill 468

Seamab Hill 439

A823

Castlehill Reservoir

Start/finish

P

1 km

N

Crown Copyright. 100031557

SEAMAB HILL

Distance	8km (5 miles) circular.
Ascent	300 metres approx.
Start and finish	Large layby on A823 at Castlehill Reservoir (GR 997033), about 3km north of Yetts of Muckhart.
Terrain	Track, hill paths and some rough ground. Boots recommended.
Map	Harveys Superwalker, the Ochil Hills.
Public transport	Limited. Reasonable bus service along the A91 to Yetts of Muckhart from Stirling or Dunfermline.
Refreshments	None on route. Nearest in Muckhart.
Toilets	None on route.

Seamab Hill is a prominent outlier of the Ochils above Glen Devon and provides an attractive and reasonably straightforward circuit with good views. Part of the hill has been acquired by the Woodland Trust, and further path development is likely in the future.

Cross the road from the layby and take the access road to Glenquey, climbing steadily. Castlehill Reservoir below was constructed in 1978 and holds 2700 million litres of water. As well as providing a supply for Fife it offers trout fishing, and is popular with anglers.

Curve left with the road and pass Glenquey House, a white cottage. Shortly after this take the track through the gate on the left into Geordie's Wood, part of the Woodland Trust area. This part of the hill is being planted with native trees, including oak, ash and rowan.

Climb steadily round the zigzags on a grassy track which gives easy walking. There is a good view back to Long Craig and Ben Thrush across Glen Devon. At another gate, leave the Woodland Trust area and enter the Forestry Commission plantation on Auchlinsky Hill. This is mainly dense conifer plantation, but the track is quite open and there is no feeling of enclosure.

Down to the right, hidden by the trees, is Glenquey reservoir (Walk 13). Ignore two tracks to the left and continue climbing steadily for about 2km. Across Glenquey is the long ridge of Innerdownie.

Approaching Seamab from Auchlinsky Hill

Leave the forest for open ground. The track ends near the top of Commonedge Hill, and a big view opens out looking south across the Forth past Kincardine Bridge. Follow a narrow path and cross the fence heading for poles stuck in the ground. Once you reach this point you should clearly see Seamab Hill ahead, with a broad ridge leading to it.

For a time you can use an ATV (all-terrain vehicle) track but after about 400 metres this keeps too far to the left and some rough ground walking is needed. You should then pick up another ATV track further to the right which leads directly towards Seamab. The view is very extensive and the flare stacks at Grangemouth can usually be seen, along with a big stretch of the Forth. The widening of the river east of Kincardine is very plain. There is a nice feeling of space.

As you near Seamab, the view takes in farmland and areas of trees below to the right with green hills ahead and to the left — a lovely prospect. Cross the fence at its highest point, where stones have been piled up to help, and re-enter the Woodland Trust area. A path leads easily up to the summit of Seamab Hill at 439m. The view is excellent, with West Lomond of Fife directly ahead. Unusually, the summit is unmarked by any form of cairn.

Farmland and forestry from the summit of Seamab

If you look down to the left from the summit, you should see a foot-bridge over the Auchlinsky Burn, but to get there, head down towards the corner of the plantation by the dyke, cross the fence and dyke and then go left along the edge of the plantation. At its corner go down a little shelf (no real path) to the bridge.

Once over the bridge a clear track develops, more or less following the forest edge above. A direct return to the start is not at present possible, but will probably be developed in time, and the route described here is an easy return for the moment. There are also longer-term plans to link the hill with Yetts of Muckhart through path development.

Cross a fence by a stile and continue. The area to the right has been planted and will grow into an attractive woodland, which should draw a good variety of birds and small mammals. It is possible that more fences will be erected but if this happens, stiles will be provided.

At the forest corner, go leftwards and then slant across the hill on a rougher path which leads over to a corner of the track you used on the outward leg. It is now an easy walk, by this track and the Glenquey road, back to the start.

WALK 14

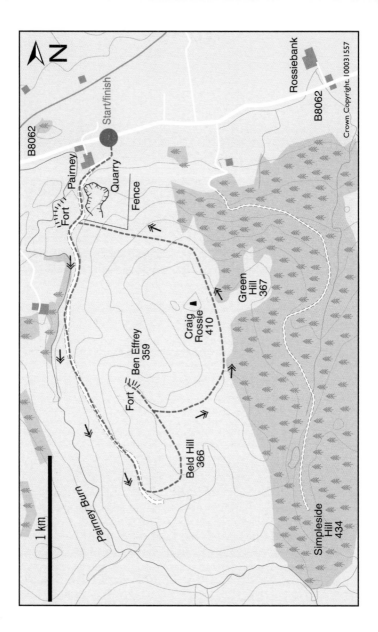

N

B8062

Start/finish

Fort
Pairney

Quarry

Fence

Fort

Ben Effrey
359

Craig
Rossie
410

Green
Hill
367

Beld Hill
366

Simpleside
Hill
434

Pairney Burn

1 km

Rossiebank

B8062

Crown Copyright 100031557

CRAIG ROSSIE

Distance	7km (4.3 miles) circular.
Ascent	350 metres approx.
Start and finish	Pairney Farm, on the B8062 road between Auchterarder and Dunning (GR 979107). There is room for 2 or 3 cars at the track end by the road. Please park considerately and do not block any entrances or gateways.
Terrain	Track, hill paths and some rough ground. Boots recommended.
Map	Harveys Superwalker, the Ochil Hills.
Public transport	None to the start. Reasonable bus services from Stirling and Perth to Auchterarder. Gleneagles Station is 5km from the start.
Refreshments	None on route. Nearest in Auchterarder.
Toilets	None on route. Nearest in Auchterarder.

Craig Rossie and Ben Effrey may not be on the Munro-bagger's litany of conquests, but these lovely wee hills, which form such a strong part of the skyline seen from the A9 below Auchterarder, provide a fine short outing with the reward of superb panoramas from their summits.

From the start, go through a kissing gate and follow the track round to the right, past the farm, and then swing left and start to climb. The track passes through a quarry. Please observe all warning notices and keep away from the quarry faces.

Continue with the track to another kissing gate, after which the going underfoot becomes grassier. The track climbs steadily with the glen of the Pairney Burn ahead. The surroundings are beautiful: farmland dotted with forestry plantations sweeps up to rounded hills in a scene that is very pleasing to the eye.

Cross Green's Burn and continue up the glen, with Ben Effrey and its small crags clearly seen up to the left. As the track rises, you can see past the hill farm of Coulshill to Steele's Knowe, a prominent outlier of the Ochils.

The track climbs more steeply for a short distance and then curves left round a hill shoulder and into the small glen of the Beldhill Burn.

You are already at the 300m contour level. At a fork, go left, straight up the hill on a rougher track.

A short, sharp climb brings you to the grassy top of Beld Hill. The name may simply mean 'bald' or it may come from the Scots 'bield', a shelter.

The views are already opening out, but get even better as you turn left and make for your first real target, Ben Effrey. There is a path of sorts most of the way across. From the 359m summit of Ben Effrey there is a superb view taking in Auchterarder, much of Strathearn and the hills beyond Crieff and Comrie. Behind you are the massed ranks of the green Ochils.

Archaeologists tell us there was an ancient fortification on Ben Effrey, which, given the view it commands, would not be surprising. It probably dates back to the Iron Age (about 700BC), but there is little sign of it on the ground now.

You can clearly see Craig Rossie: the question is, how best to get there? It is worth studying the topography for a minute or two. You have to cross, or get round, the glen holding Green's Burn. It is as easy to go back almost to Beld Hill and pick up a good path which runs over

Looking towards Auchterarder from Craig Rossie

to the forestry fence and then turns left towards Craig Rossie. The alternative is to work your way across the head of the glen, but, although you will pick up sheep tracks, this is harder work and will involve some rough ground.

Either way it will not take too long. The path crosses a small moss and then heads left, uphill on a clear traverse which leads to the col between Craig Rossie's two tops. The summit is to the right, crowned by a trig pillar at 410m. From here the view takes in Dunning, Strathearn and the country towards Perth, as well as the higher hills forming the Highland Boundary Fault.

From the westerly top you get a better view of Auchterarder and around the skyline to Ben Vorlich and Stuc a'Chroin. It is certainly a place to linger. The main top has a small plaque to Jack Simmons (1929-2003), put here by his family. A very nice place to be remembered, Jack.

So far your day has been pretty straightforward. Now for the interesting bit — getting off the hill. It's not that hard, actually, the main consideration obviously being to avoid the quarry. From the smaller top, head down the left of the ridge and you should pick up a narrow path which shoots off downhill with a pleasing directness.

It loses itself at a small gully but can be found again a little lower down. It runs about 30m left of the fence but if you miss it, you can get down easily enough by the fence line. Lower down, the path heads over to the fence and wriggles through the gorse on a reasonably scratch-free route.

The path decants you back onto the main track. Turn right and stroll down past the farm and back to your car. I am sure you will agree that these unheralded wee hills were well worth climbing.

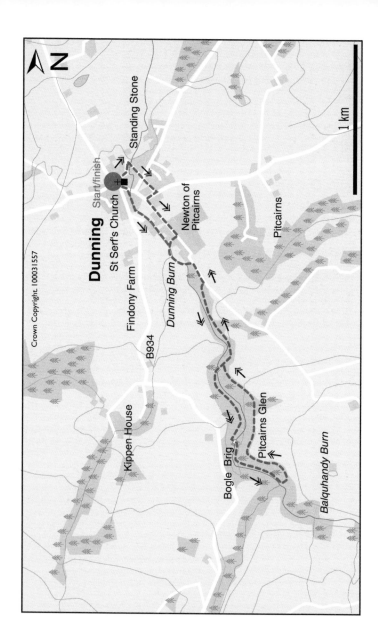

Dunning Start/finish

St Serf's Church

Standing Stone

Findony Farm

Newton of Pitcairns

Pitcairns

Dunning Burn

B934

Kippen House

Bogle Brig

Pitcairns Glen

Balquhandy Burn

Crown Copyright. 100031557

N

1 km

DUNNING AND PITCAIRNS DEN

Distance	6km (4 miles) circular.
Start and finish	The Fountain, Dunning. Park tidily in the village.
Terrain	Road, tracks and generally good paths. Boots needed in wet conditions.
Map	OS Explorer sheet 369 (Perth & Kinross).
Public transport	Docherty's bus service 20 from Stirling goes to Dunning.
Refreshments	Several pubs in Dunning.
Toilets	None on the route.
Opening hours	**St Serf's Church** (Historic Scotland) is open daily Easter to end September. The custodian will give you a first-class free guided tour.
Further information	If you visit *www.dunning.uk.net* (the excellent website of the Dunning Parish Historical Society) you can find out much more about the village and the area. The *Historic Dunning* booklet, available locally, is well worth reading before you start the walk.

The attractive and historic village of Dunning provides the basis for this walk, which as well as exploring the village itself includes the superb Pitcairns Den, truly a hidden countryside gem.

From the fountain in Dunning (given to his native village in 1874 by Alexander Martin of distant New Brunswick in Canada), walk left of the church down Kirk Wynd to the Straw House. During the intense political unrest of the early 18th century, Jacobite forces set Dunning to the torch on 28 January 1716. The story goes that the woman living in the Straw House saw what was happening and set fire to a bundle of straw inside the house. Seeing the smoke, the soldiers assumed the house had been torched and passed by. This was the only house to be saved on that terrible day.

Keep left beside the burn and continue to the field ahead to see a large standing stone. Return a short way and cross the burn by the footbridge next to the ford. Past Granco House, turn left on a path which then swings right by a large beech hedge. Turn right on Croft Terrace past the parish church. Dedicated to St Paul, it was completed in 1911 and has fine stained glass windows.

WALK 16

65

The Straw House, Dunning

At a small green, turn left (Upper Granco Street) with the war memorial to the right and at the T-junction cross to see the old well. Piped water reached the village in 1872. Turn right and at the next junction turn left (Newton of Pitcairns). The name indicates that this is a later addition to the estate of Pitcairns. There was once a thriving community of weavers here.

Newton is also known locally as 'the Dragon' after the story of the mythical beast slain by St Serf in the Den. The small wooded hill beyond it, Dun Knock, held a Pictish hill fort and is now a scheduled ancient monument.

Turn right on Well Road, passing a house with a fine outside fore stair. At the road end, turn left on the path beside the Dunning Burn — an attractive walk with plenty of trees.

The path goes left beside a wall, up steps. At the road, turn right and in 250 metres go right, through a stone archway, to regain the path into the Den. This is the start of a beautiful walk, so take your time and enjoy it to the full. The Den is part of the Pitcairns Estate, which has been owned by the Rollo family (who still live at Pitcairns House) for centuries, and it is due to their careful management that we have such a lovely place to enjoy today.

There are many fine mature trees, including in this section several hollies. The burn is initially almost invisible below. Continue with the path, getting closer to the burn, and pass a footbridge on the right. This is known as the Tory Brig, the name said to derive from it being used by Tory supporters on their way to vote in elections in times past. They wished to avoid the village as Dunning people were Whigs.

The path now widens and enters the Den proper, with the sides steepening and extending some distance above you. There were once several mills on the burn, including one in this area. Cross a footbridge and continue on the west wide of the burn. Continue to another footbridge, which you will see is called the Bogle Brig. A bogle is a Scots goblin or sprite, but the name is recent, deriving from an incident when villagers found a strange carved wooden mask near here. The mask was restored by the man who maintains the bridges and placed on a tree in the Den, and he thought it would be appropriate to name the bridge after the mask. Can you find it, I wonder?

The Den curves left, with the sides apparently ever steepening above you, until you wonder how you are going to find a way out. No need to worry. The main path ends, and a smaller path cuts steeply back up the side of the glen on a long flight of steps known as the Doig Steps after their maker. A little care may be needed here. Take your time on the ascent.

Reach the top of the glen and start the return on a higher path, a truly delightful walk through gnarled old beech and birch trees. Wander along until you reach a seat with a very romantic inscription. It commands a superb view of Strathearn and the hills beyond.

The path starts to descend gently through the old trees. At a fork keep right and use the zigzags to return to the main glen path below. Return past the Tory Brig and through the stone arch. Retrace your steps to the foot of Well Street, but carry straight on here along the roadway and then take a path on the left, beside the burn once more.

Go through a gate into a field, then through another gate, cross the burn by the footbridge beside the garage (which itself is on the site of a former mill) and walk back into the village, passing the Thorn Tree. The original tree was planted here in memory of the burning of the village in

The Bogle Brig in Pitcairns Den

1716. It lasted until 1936 when it was blown down, and a replacement tree was planted to mark the coronation of King George VI and Queen Elizabeth in 1937. This failed to thrive, as did several others, but it is hoped the current tree, planted in January 2000, will fare better.

The best of Dunning is perhaps left to last, and you should not leave without visiting the ancient St Serf's Church. The church itself, with its Romanesque steeple, dates back to the 13th century and is impressive enough, but within it is the astonishing Dupplin Cross, surely the finest Pictish monument in Scotland. It is believed to date from the 9th century, and it seems incredible, given that the cross stood outside for all that time, that so much detail of the carving has survived. It is thought that the cross may have been erected by order of King Kenneth MacAlpin as a dedication to an earlier king called Constantine.

The cross was moved to safety in the church in 2002 after restoration work had been carried out. The church custodian will tell you much more about it.

It is a miraculous survival from our ancient past and provides a fitting climax to a very satisfying outing.

CASTLE LAW

Distance	8km (5 miles) circular.
Ascent	300m approx.
Start and finish	Forgandenny. Park tidily in the village.
Terrain	Road, tracks and generally good paths. One fairly steep climb. Boots recommended.
Map	OS Explorer sheet 369 (Perth & Kinross).
Public transport	Reasonable bus service from Auchterarder to Perth via Forgandenny.
Refreshments	None on the route. Nearest in Bridge of Earn.
Toilets	None on the route.

This walk leads to in a superb hill fort with a wonderful view. It starts from the attractive village of Forgandenny, 3km west of Bridge of Earn.

Follow the road out to the east end of the village and, almost opposite the farm machinery saleroom, go right on a farm road. Pass Horselea and continue, with the steep face of the hills directly ahead. At South Dumbuils the road becomes a track and goes downhill to cross a small burn before climbing again and turning sharp left past the houses at Westhall.

Continue with the track, which is well surfaced and gives easy walking, to reach the cluster of buildings forming Glenearn. Keep right, past the farm buildings, and take the first track on the right, past a house.

When the track leads down to a small quarry, take the grass path on the right, and start climbing. Go through a gate and continue, the path becoming more of a track and heading purposefully uphill. Although you are only climbing 300m, it is a sharp ascent with little relaxation of the gradient.

The compensation comes in ever-expanding views looking across Strathearn to Moncrieffe Hill and (to its left) Kinnoull Hill, while the broad Tay also stands out clearly. The track is grassy and heads steadily uphill, passing under the power line and then cutting back sharply to the left.

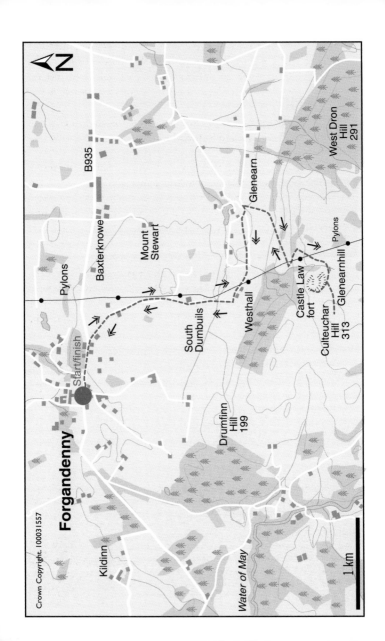

A right turn and further ascent takes you under the power line again before the gradient finally eases and the track runs on to the long-abandoned farmstead of Glenearnhill. This must have been a highly atmospheric place to live and work but you can imagine it also being harsh in the winter.

Continue past the ruined buildings for a short distance and then go right, under the trees, to find a stile which gives access to Castle Law fort. Climb up on to the fort and start exploring.

These hill forts, of which there are many in Perthshire, were always sited at strategically important points and their defences were often very powerful. Most of these forts were built about 1500-2000 years ago. As you walk around the fort, the ditch and rampart construction becomes apparent, with at least three rings of concentric defensive walls.

It would have been a very tough place to attack and therefore a place of safety for those who built it and used it as a refuge. It also commands a superb view across Strathearn and would probably have been intervisible with other forts so that signals could be passed, perhaps by fire or smoke, in case of danger. Behind the fort to the south is the main bulk of the Ochil Hills.

Castle Law from Culteuchar Hill

An alternative view of the fort can be obtained by going down to the fence corner below the fort on its south side and crossing on to Culteuchar Hill. From part-way up the hill slope, you get a good view of the fort and can appreciate the way it was designed (and also perhaps the immense labour involved in its construction). Culteuchar Hill (313m) has a trig pillar.

The return is by the same route. I had hoped to work out a circular route for this walk but this may have to wait for the second edition of the book. There is however no hardship in going back the same way.

You may see on the OS map the intriguing name 'Ecclesiamagirdle'. This is a late 17th-century tower house in a beautiful setting by a small lake. It is not on the walk and there is no access to the house, so please respect the owners' privacy.

The odd looking name, pronounced locally as 'Exmagirdle', comes from 'ecclesia', meaning a church, and a corrupted second element which may refer to a little known saint or missionary called St Gill or Gillan or possibly Grizel. There is a small ruined chapel, with graveyard, visible from the track you walk along.

Whoever this holy person was, he or she certainly chose a beautiful spot, and you can reflect on this, and on the life of the people who built the hill fort, as you stroll back along the track past Westhall and Dumbuils to Forgandenny.

GLEN LEDNOCK

Distance	6.5km (4 miles) circular.
Ascent	200 metres approx.
Start and finish	School Road car park, Comrie.
Terrain	Tracks and good paths with some rough ground. One steep descent. Boots recommended.
Map	Walks Around Comrie leaflet, available locally.
Public transport	Reasonable bus service from Perth to Comrie.
Refreshments	Reasonable choice in Comrie.
Toilets	Dalginross Bridge, Comrie.

This very varied walk includes woodland, open glen, a prominent monument and a superb waterfall. From the car park, follow the road and path east past the primary school. Cross the access road to Comrie House and, near another car park, cross the bridge over the River Lednock and turn left.

The route is initially beside the fast-flowing river, which you will see in more spectacular mode later on the walk. The path runs through attractive mixed woodland and before long starts to climb as it enters Laggan Wood. A short spur path up to the right leads to a viewpoint from which you can look across the village to Strathearn. Comrie was mainly laid out to a plan in the late 18th century. Its name comes from Gaelic words meaning a confluence or ford.

Resume the main path and continue climbing round several bends. At one point a clearing on the left gives a view across to the Melville Monument. This area was known for its oak woods in the past, but recent planting has been coniferous. Birdlife includes small raptors such as sparrow hawks and kestrels and the raucous jay, whose bright plumage you might spot. Red squirrels and roe deer also live here.

The path runs through the woodland for a considerable way, undulating gently before it begins to descend. Leaving the woods behind, the path is closer to the river and then a left turn leads across to a footbridge. This was always known as the Shakkin' Brig, as it rocked

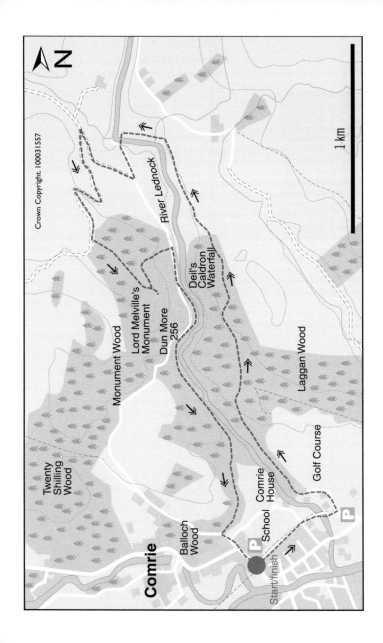

when you crossed; the current bridge is more stable, which is no doubt safer but does seem to take some of the fun away.

Walk up to the road and turn right, enjoying the views up the attractive Glen Lednock. In about 250m, go left on a clear track, climbing steadily across the open hill. This is the old Maam Road, the name coming from a word meaning a pass through the hills. There are more good views as you climb. To the right of the path, but not easy to find, is the Kinkhoast Well, whose waters were said to cure ailments including whooping cough.

At the top of the rise, look for a path on the left, back into the trees. This path climbs steadily through fairly dense woodland. It meets another path and then a short steep scramble leads you to the Melville Monument on Dun More. The 22m-high obelisk was erected in 1822 in memory of Henry Dundas, Lord Melville, one of the most powerful men in Scotland.

He was Lord Advocate from 1775 to 1783 and also held other important posts. He promoted laws which improved working conditions for the poor, and also helped to lift some of the brutal restrictions imposed after the Jacobite Rising was quashed in 1746. He died in 1811. Dundas had a country estate at Dunira, not far from here.

The view from the monument is outstanding, as befits its position at 256m, right on the Highland Boundary Fault. You look across and along Strathearn and can also see up Glen Lednock towards Ben Chonzie. Comrie's position on the fault line (which runs from Helensburgh to Stonehaven) has in the past made it liable to earth tremors, and the world's first seismometer was set up here in 1840. There is an Earthquake House at Ross, on the south side of the village.

When you are ready to leave, descend carefully back to the path junction and turn right. A steep and sometimes rough descent takes you down to the road. Turn right and soon follow the sign left to the viewing platform for the De'il's Cauldron. This spectacular waterfall was formed when the water cut a narrow passage through the rock, a type of sandstone which can fracture into blocks. The process is still continuing.

Follow the path above the river as it winds through the mature woodland. There are still oaks here, though they are no longer harvested for timber. You pass a smaller waterfall inevitably known as the Wee Cauldron, which can be seen by taking a loop path on the left.

WALK 18

Not long after this, the path leaves the river and heads off to the right, still in the woodland. This is Balloch Wood, the name (like Maam earlier) meaning a pass.

The path takes a final curve to the right and reaches the road at a gateway which can be rather muddy. Turn left and walk down Dundas Street (named for Lord Melville) back to the car park. There are other good walks around Comrie; the path leaflet will give you more detail.

The De'il's Cauldron

BEN CHONZIE

Distance	14km (9 miles) circular.
Ascent	850 metres approx.
Start and finish	Invergeldie, Glen Lednock. Take the minor road from Comrie past the Melville Monument and the De'il's Caldron and continue for 6km to an informal parking area at GR743273.
Terrain	Generally good tracks and hill paths. Some open ground. Boots essential. Take waterproofs and windproofs, map and compass and some food and drink.
Map	OS Landranger sheet 52 (Pitlochry & Crieff).
Public transport	None to the start. Reasonable bus service from Perth to Comrie.
Refreshments	None on route. Nearest in Comrie.
Toilets	None on route. Nearest in Comrie.

Ben Chonzie (also known as Ben-y-Hone) is included in this book to give readers the chance to bag a relatively straightforward Munro. The summit is at 931m (3056ft), so Ben Chonzie is not among the highest of Scotland's mountains, ranking 250th out of the 284 summits in the current Munro list, but the area surrounding it is very attractive hill country and its ascent, mostly on a good track, provides a satisfying outing without too many difficulties.

The parking area is at the junction of two old rights of way through to Loch Tay. Both are signposted, and it is the route to Ardtalnaig that you initially follow, turning right through a gate to avoid the farm buildings. There are a number of these old through routes in this area, and all of them are worth exploring if you have time and can arrange transport at the other end. The route to Ardtalnaig is 16km, so would be fairly easily accomplished in a day.

This route is followed for about 2km, crossing the Invergeldie Burn and starting to ascend steadily. You then go right, across an often dry stream bed below a small dam used to regulate the water supply. The hill track twists round several bends and begins to ascend with more of a sense of purpose. The big summit plateau of Ben Chonzie is up ahead. Over to the left is the attractive glen through which the right of way runs, with the crags of Creag na h-Iolaire (Eagle's Peak) rising above it.

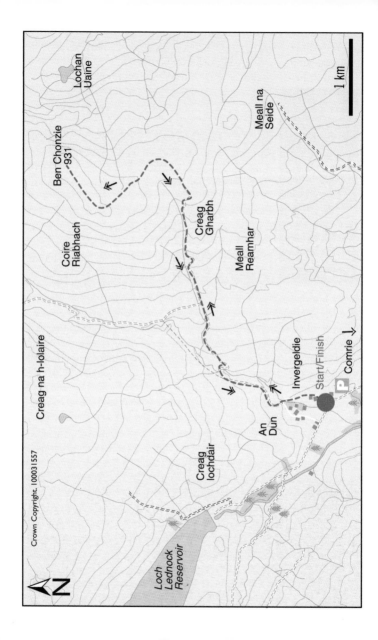

You will be lucky to spot a golden eagle, though they are found in this area, but the mewing call of a buzzard is often heard. There are deer and grouse here too, and in autumn the thrilling sound of stags calling at the rut will give your ascent an extra edge. There is another Creag na h-Iolaire over to the right and also Creag an Fhithich (Raven Peak).

Pass a side track which leads back over to the glen and continue beside a tributary burn. Beyond Creag na h-Iolaire you begin to see Creag nan Eun (hill of the birds). As you get higher, you are likely to see one of the many mountain hares for which Ben Chonzie is noted. Camouflage brown in summer with a white 'scut' at the tail, they turn white in winter.

The track is quite stony but provides straightforward walking and there are plenty of opportunities to stop and enjoy the expanding view. The track twists right and left higher up and eventually ends at a cairn. You are almost at the 800m contour here so most of the climbing is done. There is a Coire Riabhach (brindled corrie) to either side. Repetition of descriptive names like this is common in the Scottish hills.

Follow a broad, grassy path which curves left and shows signs of quad bike use. This path ascends gently to reach a line of old fence posts. Turn left and follow the posts, which are a remarkable 'handrail' guide

Looking up to Ben Chonzie

all the way to the summit, a good 2km away. If the posts should ever disappear or be removed, you need to head north-west for 1.2km then north-east for a further 800m, always keeping to the highest ground on the ridge.

The final part of the climb can seem endless, especially in mist when you have no views to enjoy, but eventually you reach a corner in the old fence which marks the summit. There is a big stone windbreak, built in the expectation of generally westerly winds and therefore not much use in a cold winter easterly!

The view takes in a huge mass of hills in almost every direction. Most are rounded tops so there is little of a dramatic nature, but it is a splendidly wild prospect. To the north-west, across Loch Tay, is the Ben Lawers group. Directly below to the north is Glen Almond and to the south-east you look into Glen Turret with its reservoir. This provides an alternative, rougher route up the hill, pathless and through shattered crags, and could also offer a way down for a circular route if you can get collected at the Loch Turret dam. This route is not advised for inexperienced walkers.

For most people, however, the return is by the way you came up. Watch carefully for the point where you leave the fence line to head over to the top of the track. Once you have hit the cairn, it is very easy walking down and you can enjoy the surroundings to the full, happy to have bagged your Munro.

The top of the track leading up to Ben Chonzie

COWDEN

Distance	10km (6 miles) circular.
Start and finish	Field of Refuge car park, Comrie (south side of the bridge).
Terrain	Road, tracks and paths. Sections likely to be muddy. Boots recommended.
Map	Walks Around Comrie leaflet, available locally.
Public transport	Reasonable bus service from Perth to Comrie.
Refreshments	Reasonable choice in Comrie.
Toilets	Dalginross Bridge, Comrie.

This walk includes farmland, woods and a lengthy stretch of the River Earn. Sections of it can be rather muddy and you are almost certain to encounter cattle, so dogs must be kept under close control.

From the car park, cross the main road and walk along Strowan Road, with the river on your left. Continue with the road past the fire station, bend right and follow the road all the way to its end. Cross, and take the signposted path through the wood.

This is known as the Bishop's Planting and contains some fine mature trees. At the end of the wood, turn right along a narrow strip of trees and walk out to the road. Turn left, and follow the signposted, narrow path between fences on the far side of the road (not the road itself, which leads to Cowden House).

Where the road bends left, go ahead through a gate and up a short slope to another gate. This is the first muddy section and you will often find cattle here. Walk across the field, still climbing, and go through another gate, bearing right to pick up a clearer track which is in fact part of the old route out of Comrie towards Braco, long supplanted by the present B827 road. The track is grassy but sections can also be rather muddy. On the left is the site of the long-abandoned Bogton Farm and further left you can see Cowden Loch.

The track bends left and runs out to the B827. Turn left along Glascorrie Road (the name means 'green glen'). The road is shaded by trees including oak and alder, with the Newton Burn to the right. In

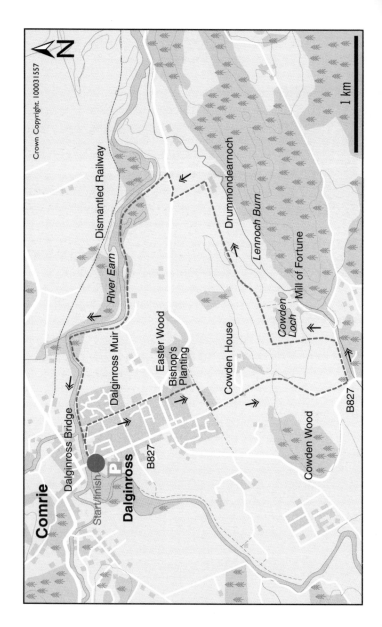

Cowden Loch

about 400m, turn left on a track as signed and almost immediately left again on another track which climbs gradually.

Follow this track to its end, passing a small pond, and then go through a gate and along the field edge by the fence. In about 200m, go right on a clearer path which runs through the fields, across the hill slope. There is a view of Cowden Loch to the right. In winter you may well see a variety of wildfowl here. Beyond the loch is the site of an old meal mill called Mill of Fortune.

Pass through several gates, keeping on the path which is well signed, and pass a large knoll, walking for a short time beside a conifer plantation. After this you pick up a fenced farm track which gradually improves as you walk towards the farm of Drummondearnoch ('the place on the ridge above the Earn'). There are views of wooded hills to the right as you walk along.

Go through the farm and turn left along its access road, which is lined with tall birches. At the South Crieff Road, turn right. Walk on the right, facing the traffic. In about 400m, turn left at the signpost (which rather optimistically says 'Comrie 1½' — it's a bit further than that) and walk across the field to a stile to pick up the riverside path.

WALK 20

The Earn is now followed all the way back to Comrie, but the path is often a little way from the river and the tree cover means the water cannot always be seen. The Earn carries a good variety of birdlife which, in season, may include sandpipers, goosanders, mallard and heron. The first field you cross may have Highland cattle in it. I have always found them walker-friendly, but dogs should be kept on a tight lead.

Beyond this field the path enters an area of mixed woodland. As you enter the wood, you have to cross an unbridged burn, but it is normally quite easy. Trees include birch, rowan and alder, and much of the ground is wet and marshy. This type of woodland is called 'carr'. There are old gravel workings in this area. Gravel is often taken from rivers, but the extraction needs to be carefully controlled in order to avoid undue bank erosion.

The path is of variable quality but always easy to follow. Some parts may be a little overgrown and there is a feeling of remoteness. The river bends to the left and you see Fairness Farm ahead as you follow field edges along on a thin path.

Pass a sewage treatment works. The river is now close by, and the path improves along a field edge. Soon you see the houses of Comrie ahead, and in the distance is the Melville Monument on Dun More. The river (mostly hidden by trees again) makes a big bend to the left.

Follow a wonderful row of old, gnarled beech trees, once probably part of a hedge, a long time ago. At a fork go right, staying in the trees, close to the river. Go through a gate at the first houses and continue with the path until, at a wall corner, a sign points left. Walk out to the road and turn right past the Fire Station back to the car park.

The River Earn near Comrie

THE BEST OF CRIEFF (1)

Distance	7km (4.5 miles) circular.
Start and finish	Taylor Park car park, Crieff.
Terrain	Road, tracks and good paths. Boots only needed in wet conditions.
Map	Crieff Paths leaflet available locally.
Public transport	Good bus services to Crieff from Perth and Stirling.
Refreshments	Good choice in Crieff.
Toilets	In the town centre.
Further information	The Tourist Information Centre in Crieff (01764 652578) is open all year.

Crieff is an attractive town with a good range of facilities; it also has an outstandingly good footpath network. Any of the waymarked walks is worth taking, but the selection described here and in Walk 22 picks out some of the highlights of the area through a process of 'mix and match'.

From the car park, cross the bridge over the Turret Burn and immediately turn left, signposted for Laggan Hill via Lady Mary's Walk. Follow this lovely shady path beside the burn which burbles away on your left.

Pass through the piers of an old railway bridge. There may be a short diversion after this as the riverside path has been closed due to erosion, but it is soon regained and before long swings right to join the broad River Earn below old beech trees.

Cross a small 'beach' and go up to join the wide Lady Mary's Walk at a signpost. The walk was named for Lady Mary Murray in 1825 by her father, Sir Patrick Murray of Ochtertyre, who owned the land, and it has been open to the public ever since. Lady Mary loved to walk here and it is easy to see why.

You soon reach the first of a series of intriguing carved seats. This one has the initials HG and KB and the romantic inscription: 'Graven in beechwood, our true love's sign of promises trothed and hearts entwined.' With your heart uplifted by this, continue along, the serene old gnarled trees and the broad river making a perfect scene.

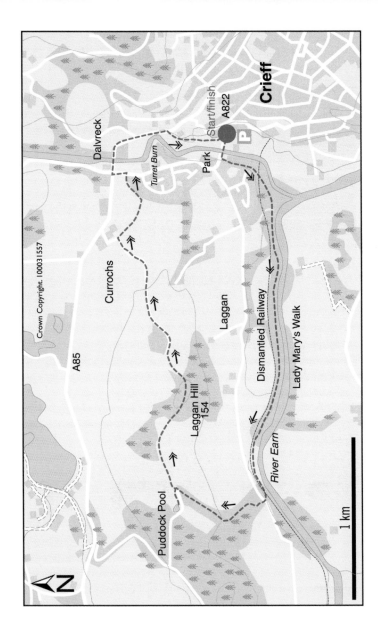

Pass the second seat, with an inscription relating to the former railway line: 'The tumbling bridge and fallow field, once deeply scarred by soot and steel, now Nature has crept in to heal.' Then the third, which is backless, and reads: 'Bright flashes rouse the salmon's sleep, silently fanning the shadowed deep — and up he leaps!'

The fourth seat, with a view of the distant monument to Sir David Baird, has a reference to Ling-a-Wing, which was a local name for a popular bathing spot on the river.

Pass a retaining wall and continue beside a calm stretch of the river to the fifth seat. It speaks of: 'Blue plumed doves, murmuring low', and there are indeed wood pigeons to be heard around here.

At a waymark, go right through the railway bridge and at the next signpost, go right again. You are now briefly on an old droving road. Crieff was one of the most important cattle markets in the 18th and 19th centuries and thousands of head of livestock would have come this way.

In 60 metres, turn left at the signpost for Laggan Hill. At first the grassy path appears to be heading in the wrong direction but it then twists sharply back right to a gate. Just beyond the gate is a seat with a lovely view over Crieff to Strathearn and the Ochils.

The River Earn from Lady Mary's Walk

WALK 21

Continue climbing steadily and at a junction go left for about 200 metres to see the Puddock Pool, almost hidden in the woods. Puddock is the Scots name for a frog. Return along the track (one of the old Ochtertyre Estate carriageways) and continue with a former hedge to the right, now grown into trees. There are glimpses of the hills to your left.

Reach an unexpected carved seat with another romantic verse: 'Here I sought my girlhood's dream and pledged my heart's desire, Amid the mountainsides and streams of bonny Ochtertyre.' After this, you climb to the highest point on the hill then start descending gently. Another seat with a lovely view asks 'Pray tell Lady Mary, where did you go?' – a question to which we may never know the answer.

Shortly after this turn left at a signpost (blue arrow, Currochs Walk) and follow the path by the dyke through a kissing gate (designed for very slim people!). The path winds easily down to Currochs, beautifully set with great views of the hills. At a gate turn right along the field edge and in 50m look carefully for a marker and gate on the left. This marker can get obscured by vegetation in summer.

Carved seat on Lady Mary's Walk

Looking north to Glen Turret from Laggan Hill

Follow the markers across the field then down to a gate (there are often cattle here). Go through into an odd little strip of young trees where the path has to dodge about. Reach Turretbank Road and turn left. At the A85 turn right and cross the Turret Burn.

Follow the road round a sharp right bend and in about 200 metres look for a metal gate on the right, helpfully labelled 'Park'. Go through and turn left on a surfaced path below a wall.

At a fork go right and at a floral 'roundabout' go right, down the steps. Cross the footbridge over the burn and turn left, back to the car park.

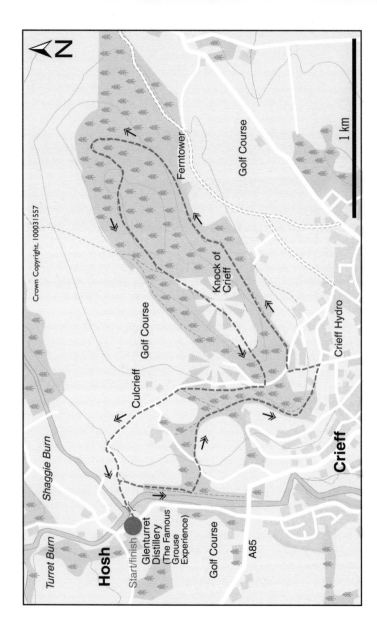

THE BEST OF CRIEFF (2)

Distance	9.5km (5.5 miles) circular.
Start and finish	Glenturret Distillery (the Famous Grouse Experience). Turn off A85 just west of Crieff as signed and follow the minor road for 800m to the car park on the right.
Terrain	Road, tracks and generally good paths. Boots recommended.
Map	Crieff Paths leaflet available locally.
Public transport	Good bus service to Crieff from Stirling and Perth.
Refreshments	Good choice in Crieff. Restaurant at the Distillery Visitor Centre.
Toilets	At the distillery and in Crieff town centre.
Opening hours	The Famous Grouse Experience at **Glenturret Distillery** is open daily (except Christmas and New Year's Day), 9am-6pm. Last tour 4.30pm. More limited hours may apply in winter. More details from 01764 656565 or *www.thefamousgrouse.com*.

This walk links Scotland's oldest distillery with a lovely hill above Crieff which offers outstanding views.

From the distillery, walk through the car park towards the shop and restaurant and look for the footpath sign. Note the statue of Towser the cat, who in a career spanning 24 years caught over 28,000 mice and earned herself an entry in the *Guinness Book of Records*.

Cross the Brig o'Dram footbridge over the Turret Burn and follow the path uphill into the wood, and then back to the right. At the signpost go right. You are following red arrows for the next section. The path stays above the turbulent burn through woodland.

In about 400 metres, turn left at a signpost (Culcrieff ½), and climb steadily through lovely mature woods round several bends to reach a minor road. Turn left with views of hills to the left. At a cross-path, keep ahead with Culcrieff Golf Course to the left to reach the houses at Culcrieff (part of Crieff Hydro Estate).

Just before the houses, turn right on a track. At the 3rd tee, keep left and stay on the main track as it contours round the hill. To the right is a wide view taking in Ochtertyre House and the hills beyond.

At a multiple signpost keep right on a broad track which continues round the hill, a lovely walk, then re-enters woodland.

Pass houses, with views down to the town below, and reach a road. At a gateway, turn left uphill as signed. Through the gate is Crieff Hydro, one of a number of similar establishments set up in the 19th and early 20th century when 'hydropathic remedies' using mineral-rich water were very fashionable. There were once over twenty Hydros in Scotland. Those that remain, such as Crieff and Dunblane, are now hotels.

Walk up the field to another gate and then follow the road past holiday lodges to reach a small car park. Turn right here, leaving the red route, and follow the road for about 250 metres until you see a sign for the Knock Circular Path. Follow this track along the edge of the wood.

There are big views east and south across Strathearn to the Ochil Hills, and you can even see the two Lomonds of Fife. Re-enter the woods. At a Crieff Hydro Estate sign keep ahead on the broad firm track. Crieff Golf Course is to the right.

Past a Millennium Cairn, dated 1.1.2000, the track starts climbing gently with tall conifers to the left and before long, a felled area to the right. Looking right you can see Milquhanzie Hill, which holds an old hillfort, and again there is an extensive view across Strathearn.

The track continues to rise and twists sharply back left, then swings right and levels out. Look out for a sign pointing left to Knock summit, and take this path. The rough path curves right and climbs steadily. After a short, stiff ascent you reach a cairn at the actual 279m summit of the Knock. There are no views, but keep going, the best is yet to come!

Follow the path along the ridge (it can be very dark here). A short, rough descent follows, then you pick up blue arrows. Go through a gate and turn left. Cross an area of light woodland and climb again to reach the Knock Viewpoint at 242m. There is a view indicator dedicated to Robert Rule and inscribed 'I will lift up mine eyes unto the hills from whence cometh my help.' It is certainly a wonderful panorama.

To the north and west the view takes in Ben Chonzie, the other hills around Glen Turret, Ben Vorlich and Stuc a'Chroin and the Melville Monument above Glen Lednock. To the south is Strathearn

WALK 22

92

View from the Knock

and the Ochils. You may pick out Craig Rossie. Further east are the Fife Lomonds.

When you are ready to leave, continue with the path in the same direction (still with blue arrows) through attractive woodland with birches, aspen and rowan trees. Descend steadily into denser woods.

Pass two seats and at a fork, go right on a lovely wee path which leads you easily down to a road. Turn right. You now pick up red arrows again, forking left to follow a road mainly downhill for about a kilometre.

At Culcrieff Golf Centre go straight on (not left with the road) past the Hydro Activity Centre and onto a stony track. This track descends steadily and bends left into woods which include superb old beeches.

At a sharp bend go left on the path as signed and follow it down, back to the Brig o'Dram and the distillery. A distillery tour will round off your day nicely. Glenturret is Scotland's oldest distillery, founded in 1775, and the tour explains many of the mysteries of the production of whisky (Gaelic *uisquebaugh*, the water of life) and includes a tasting at the end. As you leave don't forget to give a wave to the 5m copper statue of Lady Grouse herself.

WALK 22

93

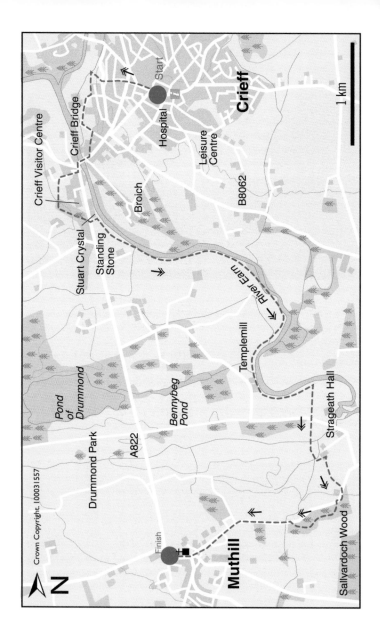

CRIEFF TO MUTHILL

Distance	9km (5.5 miles) linear.
Start	James Square, Crieff (ample parking nearby).
Finish	Muthill. Return by bus.
Terrain	Road, tracks and generally good paths. Some stretches may be muddy. Boots or strong shoes recommended.
Map	Crieff Walks leaflet available locally.
Public transport	Regular buses from Muthill to Crieff (Stagecoach service 47).
Refreshments	Wide choice in Crieff. Café and inns in Muthill.
Toilets	At the start and at Crieff Visitor Centre.
Further information	**Stuart Crystal** and the **Crieff Visitor Centre** are both open all year. For times enquire locally. Both have cafes and toilets.

This walk, a substantial part of which is along the River Earn, offers a variety of scenery and makes a very pleasant outing. The initial section getting you out of Crieff needs a little care. You are following yellow markers (the River Earn Walk) so keep an eye out for these along the way.

From the handsome fountain in James Square (erected to mark the beneficence of the Murrays of Ochtertyre) walk west along the main road. Continue into Lodge Street and cross the A822 into Drummawhandie Road. Cross the next road and go down steps. At Ryan Place, cross to a path into playing fields.

Walk along the right edge of the field to pick up a path which curves left and drops down below a high bank. The path runs past more playing fields. Cross a road and continue with the path to pass a cemetery.

At the cemetery gates, turn right (Earnbank Road, a narrow lane). On the left is the Catholic church, which has good stained glass (but don't turn left here). Continue ahead along an attractive lane through houses which show a real architectural mix. Reach the main road, turn right and cross the Earn. There is a fine view to the right up to the Glen Turret hills.

Turn right on Alichmore Lane, noting the house with the outside fore stair. At the end of the lane, turn left along the field edge. At the next gate you will find the first of a number of wooden carvings which celebrate various aspects of water along the route. This one tells the story of the Water Pipe Arm. Rather than detailing these little stories, I will leave you to read them for yourself.

At the top of the ride, turn left into Thomas Wood. Note the lack of undergrowth, typical of a beech wood. Walk through the lovely old trees, watching carefully for a left turn marker. Walk down to the road opposite Stuart Crystal. The Crieff Visitor Centre is just to the left.

Cross the road and go through the Stuart Crystal car park to pick up the riverside path. The Earn is followed for the next 3.5km of the walk. It is a noted salmon river, and fish of more than 4kg (10lbs) are not uncommon. You will almost certainly see anglers trying their luck.

The next gate tells of the Horse Mussel Filter Trough, a Roman device. The path runs through trees and bushes for a time. Cross a footbridge, go through a gate and along a field edge. In summer you will find many different wild flowers along here.

Swans and cygnets on the Earn

Where the riverbank broadens out, stay by the fence on an undefined path for about 300m before picking up the riverside path again. The next gate depicts the Trolling Shirt used by poachers. Keep by the fence as the bank again widens out, and pass an island in the river.

The Earn bends to the right. Keep following the fence, picking up bits of path. The next gate story is the Shepherd's Stilts. There is a lovely view looking back here.

Reach Templemill farm where the river bends sharply left. A footpath goes right, to Bennybeg, but you stay by the river. Note the story of the Miller's Flow on the gate.

Follow field edges along, on the flood bank. The Earn can be tempestuous and has caused widespread flooding on numerous occasions, especially lower down towards Bridge of Earn.

Reach the piers of a former railway bridge (a long-disused branch line) and turn right at the Heron Hook Shovel gate to walk below the old line. In 200m go up onto the line and under a bridge to walk through a cutting. This section may be quite muddy. Turn left (on a very muddy track) to Strageath Hall. Turn right and follow the access track out to a minor road.

Walking by the Earn

Turn right here and in 60m turn left as signed into Sallyardoch Wood. Watch carefully in about 150m for a narrow path off to the right, and follow this path as it winds through the tall pines. This is a delightful stroll. At the end of the wood, rejoin the road for the final stretch into Muthill (pronounced Mooth-ill, by the way, not Mut-hill). The road carries little traffic and you soon reach pavement as you enter the village.

Muthill is an attractive wee place with a long history. At a fork keep left then go right past the primary school to reach the old parish church, now in the care of Historic Scotland. The tower is 12th century and the church, which at one time shared status with Dunblane Cathedral, may have been founded by Celtic monks known as Culdees. It was abandoned in the 1820s when the present parish church was built. (St James', opposite the primary school, is the oldest Episcopal church in the area, built 1836.)

The old church is open in summer months and makes a lovely place to sit and reflect on the walk you have just enjoyed.

Muthill Old Church

KINNOULL HILL

Distance	7km (4.5 miles) circular.
Start and finish	Quarry car park, Corsiehill (signposted from the A85 in Perth via Manse Road and Hatton Road).
Terrain	Tracks and good paths. One fairly steep climb. Boots only needed in wet conditions.
Map	Free Kinnoull Hill path leaflet available locally.
Public transport	Buses to Perth Bridge, about 1.5km from the start.
Refreshments	Wide choice in Perth.
Toilets	None on the route.

Kinnoull Hill Woodland Park, above Perth, comprises a large area of mixed woodland and has an extensive path network. This walk combines two of the park areas to give a satisfying figure-of-eight outing.

From the car park in the old quarry (last worked in the 1920s), climb the steps and turn right (red marker) to walk down to a bend in the road. Take the clear path past the yellow warning sign (for steep slopes).

Keep left at a fork in 100m, climbing steadily, and keep right at the next fork, still following red markers. The path winds through mature natural woodland which holds a good variety of birdlife. There is a multiplicity of paths in this area, so keep a careful eye on the markers.

Keep right at another fork and pass a small brick building. Continue on a narrower path through mature pines and beech. The path runs along a small shelf to reach a field edge. At the right turn for Barnhill, keep straight ahead, now on a clearer path. Join another path: the climb proper now starts!

The path goes left for about 200m, then right at a picnic table with a limited view over Perth. Climb quite steeply uphill for a time. The slope soon eases. Turn right as signed and follow the path up to reach the Stone Table. Erected by the 9th Earl of Kinnoull, it commands a superb view down the Tay and across to the Fife Lomonds. The vertical face below is part of a fault, and the volcanic rock supports a wide range of plants. Thyme grows around the area of the table.

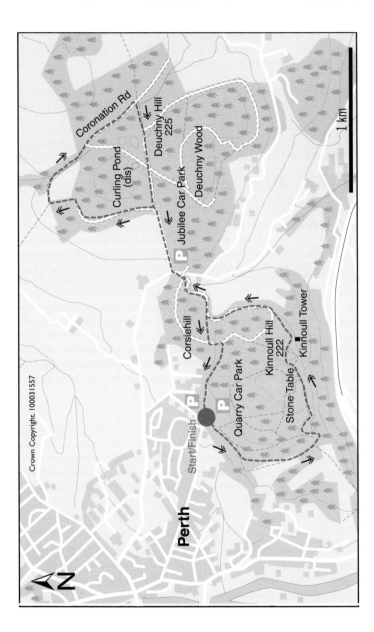

Moncrieffe Hill from Kinnoull Hill

A short path leads to the trig pillar and view indicator on Kinnoull Hill. Although only at 222m, the view is wide, taking in a wonderful hill panorama. The indicator was erected in 1948 to mark the 25th anniversary of the gift of this land to Perth by Lord Dewar.

Return to the Stone Table and turn left (Nature Walk) to follow the edge of the cliffs round a gully and up to Kinnoull Tower. This too was built for the 9th Earl, in imitation of castles he had seen above the Rhine in Germany. It is called a 'folly' as it was built to look like an ancient ruin. Wallflowers and foxgloves grow on the stonework.

From the Tower, follow the surfaced path. This is part of a growing network of 'all ability' trails in the Woodland Park, constructed to give people with limited mobility or in wheelchairs as many recreational opportunities as possible.

At a fork, go right, and continue on the wide track above the valley of the Deuchny Burn, through tall beeches which form a remarkable avenue like a natural cathedral. Turn right along the edge of the wood with a view down to the Tay. Reach, and cross, the Jubilee car park, and turn right at the field edge (Jubilee Walk, also used by horses). Follow the track, climbing gently. Reach a gate and turn left into conifer forest. The path curves right, then you turn left (at point 5) through a plantation of larch and pine.

The path again curves right, with a view over Scone below. Go through two gates, cross the field and walk along the far edge below the

A shady woodland path on Kinnoull Hill

trees. You have now joined the Coronation Road, an ancient highway used by Scottish kings and nobles travelling from Falkland Palace in Fife to Scone Palace. King Charles II, the last to be crowned at Scone, came this way, probably with a large retinue, in 1651.

This section of path may be rather muddy. Cross the Langley Burn, after which the path improves and climbs to re-enter the forest. Keep on the main track and in about 450m, turn right as signed onto a sharp rise over Deuchny Hill. At the top of the rise, join a broad track. Just past the double junction, a short path on the right leads to an old curling pond, long disused and now a rich habitat for rushes and water lilies.

Continue along the main track, retracing your steps to the Jubilee car park. Walk through the car park, cross the road (which is part of National Cycle Route 77) and fork right (red arrows) by a gate past Forest Lodge. You will probably see squirrels in this area, their presence often indicated by discarded half-eaten pine cones.

Follow the broad all-abilities path, which curves left. About 100m after a track comes in from the left, turn right (red and yellow arrows). The path winds pleasantly through tall trees, crosses a footbridge and narrows. At the T-junction, turn right and follow the quarry fence down to the view indicator on Corsiehill.

This too commands a sumptuous view of the big hills to the north and is a place to pause. When you are ready to leave, take the path to the left of the indicator, down to the car park and the end of the walk.

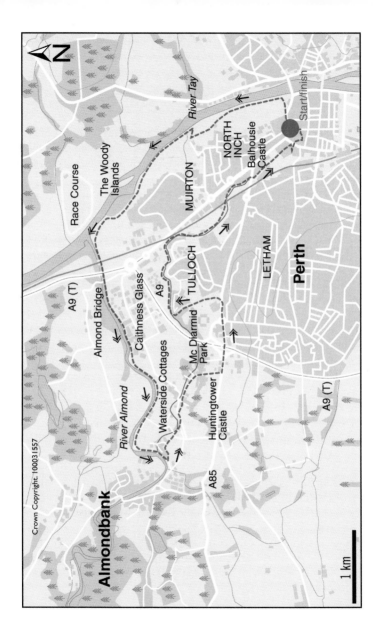